Murray

Sports or Athletics:
A North American Dilemma

PROCEEDINGS OF THE 15th ANNUAL UNIVERSITY OF
WINDSOR SEMINAR ON CANADIAN-AMERICAN RELATIONS
HELD AT THE UNIVERSITY OF WINDSOR, WINDSOR, ONTARIO

1973

Edited by
J. ALEX MURRAY
University of Windsor

CANADIAN-AMERICAN SEMINAR
University of Windsor
Windsor, Ontario

Printed for the Canadian-American Seminar
by Herald Press Limited

PREFACE

Athletics, since earliest Greek times, has been associated with competitive activities based upon clear-cut outcomes, direct rewards and, above all, opportunities for contest before admiring spectators. Sport, on the other hand, is athletics' simpler and less clearly defined, but infinitely exhilarating, precursor. Today, North Americans may be alienating themselves from their sports' birthright by becoming polarized into an inert mass of spectators and an adulated minority of participants.

Out of this polarization, a multi-million dollar industry has emerged. The scope of this commercial enterprise cannot help but have far-reaching social and political repercussions.

The primary question to be asked is whether athletics as our dominant form of sports is engulfing and pre-empting all other forms. Our failure to face the social reality of this possibility creates formidable consequences. The competitive spirit, with its assertion of individualism, is being suffocated by a belief that a standardized, predictable product is both a winning and a paying one. Athletics has lost its uniqueness to become an extension of technology; athletes have become the faceless components in a commercial or ideological machine.

It was the purpose of this Seminar to explore the widening gulf between sport and athletics, and to endeavor to examine and predict trends in the United States and Canada. The 1973 Seminar was innovative in many respects, a special motion picture which depicted the many facets and dimensions of sports and athletics introduced the topic. At the same time, we were able to secure experts who took opposing views on many issues that were raised. The excitement and interests which were generated during the two day Seminar were fostered by the speeches reproduced in this text. For those who were unable to attend the Seminar these proceedings will provide an accurate account of the arguments and positions taken by the different participants. At all times the original positions taken by the different panelists is reproduced as faithfully as possible so that their frames of reference are neither obscured nor distorted.

The Canadian-American Seminar is the only annual conference which focuses on contemporary social issues that affect the lives of North Americans. Each year the Advisory Board of the Seminar selects a topic which they consider to be of current interest and concern to Canadians and Americans. "Sport or Athletics: A North American Dilemma," was the unanimous choice of the board, and with the assistance of the Faculty of Physical Health and Education at the University of Windsor, the 1973 Seminar achieved its anticipated goal of an open forum in which the pros and cons of the topic area were discussed and questioned in an intelligent and thought-provoking manner. The Canadian-American Seminar thanks all those speakers who made this possible by their participation.

A Seminar of this scope and depth demanded the unlimited cooperation of many people. Professors Richard Moriarty and James Duthie were outstanding in their contribution by helping to formulate from the very beginning the scope and focus of this particular conference, and in advising the Director and Seminar staff in particular facets of this Seminar. Their contribution is recognizable throughout the total Seminar, and we appreciate very much their input. Also, a note of thanks and acknowledgement is gratefully extended to a few special members of the Seminar staff who worked tirelessly on this program. Professors William Arison, Mary Gerace, and Marge Holman were extremely helpful in organizing the many details which made the 1973 Seminar the success attributed to all who attended. I would be remiss if I did not give a special note of thanks again this year to my secretary Lea Wilkinson. As a full-time member of the Canadian-American Seminar staff, she directs with the utmost efficiency the day-to-day activities which culminate in the November conference. I sincerely thank her for her efforts.

The errors that might appear in these proceedings are mine and reluctantly I must accept the responsibility for them all.

July 1, 1974   J. Alex Murray
Windsor, Ontario, Canada   Director

SPORT OR ATHLETICS: A NORTH AMERICAN DILEMMA

FIFTEENTH ANNUAL UNIVERSITY OF WINDSOR CANADIAN-AMERICAN SEMINAR

LIST OF CONTRIBUTORS

"TOO MUCH SPORT TO BE BUSINESS OR TOO MUCH BUSINESS TO BE SPORT?"

THE FRANK BOLAND MEMORIAL LECTURE

"THE NORTH AMERICAN SYNDROME: SPORT FOR ADULTS—ATHLETICS FOR CHILDREN"

"ATHLETICS AND THE BIG DOLLAR"

"SPORT OR ATHLETICS: A CONCEPTUAL ANALYSIS"

James Keating
> *Professor of Philosophy*
> DePaul University

John McMurtry
> *Professor of Philosophy*
> University of Guelph

Bil Gilbert
> *Editorial Staff*
> "Sports Illustrated"

> **Gerald Kenyon, (Chairman)**
> *Dean, Faculty of Human Kinetics*
> *and Leisure Studies*
> University of Waterloo

James Keating
Professor of Philosophy
DePaul University

I honestly approach our subject with a sense of real excitement and anticipation because you Canadians must have made some remarkable breakthrough which, until now, you have kept secret. It was only a few years ago, in 1969 to be exact, that a distinguished Canadian Task Force reluctantly decided that they really couldn't determine *what sport really is* or, in fact, *what a sport is.*

Yet during the next two days we will presumably and hopefully be comparing this great unknown (Sport) with Athletics. That's what it's all about isn't it? Sport Or Athletics: A North American Dilemma. Yet who has recently provided us with the necessary functional or operational definition of sport which will permit us to compare it with athletics? Basic terms such as "sport," "play," "game," "competition" have been extended by common and careless usage to the point of meaninglessness. "Sport," as I view it today, defies useful functional definition because, through usage it has become a generic term embracing various species, the two most prominent of which are athletics and play. Since only specific terms admit of precise definition, it is impossible to define a generic term like freedom, justice or love which encompasses various species. Thus, if there is a genuine North American Dilemma, it would seem to me to be Play or Athletics rather than Sport or Athletics. Yet, I'm not convinced that this is a true dilemma. I see no reason why we can't have the best of both worlds. In other words, there is no reason why we can't have both play and athletics. Our problem is not to confuse them or treat them as synonyms. We must come to recognize the radical distinction between these two types of activities and to keep them in their proper place and perspective.

In writing an article entitled SPORTSMANSHIP AS A MORAL CATEGORY,[1] it was obvious that its development entailed the definition of the word "sportsmanship." What, then, is sportsmanship? Well, sportsmanship is the attitude and conduct becoming a sportsman. And who is a sportsman? One who is interested in or takes part in sport. And what, pray tell, is sport? Sport, Webster

1. *Ethics,* LXXV (October, 1964) pp. 25-35.

tells us is "that which diverts and makes mirth", it is an "amusement, recreation, pastime." My problem then was to determine the conduct and attitude proper to this type of activity and this can be done only after a more careful consideration of the nature of sport. Remember, sport, according to the great lexicographer is pleasant diversion, recreation, amusement, pastime. But how relevant is Webster today? Is this how you would describe the World Series, the Stanley Cup, the Masters, the Davis Cup, the Super Bowl or the Grey Cup? In fact, is this even the way you would describe a high-school hockey or basketball championship? Do the "sport" pages of our newspapers detail the pleasant diversion and amusements of the citizenry, or are they preoccupied with regional, national and international contests which capture the imaginations, the emotions and the pocketbooks of millions of fans? It is precisely at this point that we come face to face with a basic problem. Because the term *sport* has been loosely applied to radically different types of human behavior, because it is naively regarded as an apt description of 1) activity which seeks only pleasant diversion and, on the other hand, 2) of the agonistic struggle to demonstrate personal or group excellence, the determination of the conduct proper to a participant in "sport" becomes a sticky business indeed.

It is my contention, then, that the term "sport" as it is commonly used is so hopelessly ambiguous that its usage precludes any meaningful discussion or communication. It is, however, so deeply engrained in language, not only English but French, German, etc., as well that any attempt to expunge it would be quixotic. We have "sport" pages and "sport" writers and commentators and "sport" programs. When I talk with the fellows at the corner bar I use the term "sport" as promiscuously as the next fellow. When we are meeting however in an international conference, as alleged experts, both theoretical and practical, and when we are carefully considering the merits and dangers in certain types of human activity, then we should be more precise. We should make some attempt to sharpen up our terminology.

As far back as 1967, I had given up on my original sport v. athletics dichotomy. Yet despite innumerable talks, debates and an occasional published article, I was successful in convincing very few scholars of the value of the new distinction (play v. athletics). Imagine, then, my surprise and delight when I stumbled upon the Report of the Task Force on Sports for Canadians, published in 1969. On the very first page of the preamble, we find refreshing honesty in the state of the initial difficulties that confronted them. I am reading from the preamble. "What is sport? The temptation is to reply almost any human activity. Take such unusual or exotic pursuits as parachute jumping, water skiing, drag racing, demolition derbys, croquet, chess, rifle shooting, thoroughbred racing, scuba diving, fishing derbys. . . . The diversity of what can be called sporting activity is amazing." The Task Force then continues with shocking candor. "After such a canvass we can appreciate why we have no neat definitions of what sport really is or what sport is."[2] Had the authors been less perceptive, less deeply rooted in concrete existential experience, they may have gone the way of Paul Weiss and defined sport as "a traditionalized set of rules to be exemplified by men who try to be excellent in and through their bodies."[3] They escape this simplistic pitfall as a result of their sound conviction that they were grappling with a vast array of human activities, many of which were far removed from all pursuit of excellence. The members of the Task Force were struggling gallantly, if blindly, to embrace in their definition of sport; human activities which are normally non-competitive as well as those of a highly competitive nature. It was only natural that they would eventually succumb to the temptation to identify sport with athletics.

Now since I hold that athletics and play are two distinct species under the genus "sport" and that they are easily distinguishable and radically diverse types of human activity, I should be prepared to offer what I have characterized as functional definitions of each. First, consider athletics. Athletics are physical contests designed to determine human excellence through an honorable victory in a contest. Thus they are competitive by their very nature. Professional football, baseball, basketball and hockey are excellent examples of athletic contests. So, also, are the various Olympic contests, intercollegiate and interscholastic contests. In fact, even most of the highly organized Little League contests must be regarded as athletics. Play, on the other hand, is a free creative activity in which the goal of the participants is to maximize the joy of the moment, seeking no goal outside the activity itself.

To clarify this point, let us begin with a brief look at playful activities and then compare them with athletic contests. Are golf, tennis, baseball, basketball, etc., playful activities? They certainly

2. *Ethics,* LXXV (October, 1964) p. 2.
3. "Sport: A Philosophic Inquiry," *Southern Illinois University Press,* 1969, p. 143.

can be and frequently are. The intention and attitude of the participants are the crucial determinants. The primary purpose of the person who truly plays is to enjoy the activity itself, to maximize the pleasure or joy of the moment. In order to do so, he may try hard to win and if he does so fine. If he loses, however, so what, as long as the activity itself was enjoyable.

Many activities originate as games to be played for the mere pleasure and joy which they evoke. They are, however, almost imperceptibly, converted into agonistic contests in which the playful spirit is totally absent and the prime purpose of the activity soon becomes the determination of a winner. Such contests often have as an important auxiliary function, the entertainment of spectators. Unlike the person engaged in genuine play the athlete's objective is not to maximize the joy of the moment. Like the political candidate and the attorney in a court case, the aim of the athlete is honorable victory in the contest. When the tide of battle is running in his favor, he may experience great pleasure in the proceedings themselves, but this is merely incidental to the end of the contest. Thus the athlete is engaged in a physical contest governed by rules which have as their main purpose the determination of excellence and often, but only secondarily, the involvement and consequent excitement of the spectators.

Many knowledgeable experts have made the same mistake of identifying sport with athletics or, at least, failing to make many meaningful distinctions between the two terms.

A prime example occurred several years ago when the staff members of *Sports Illustrated* endorsed a startling suggestion. It called for a one month moratorium on sport. "No baseball, no football, no basketball, no hockey, no sports pages, nothing." No sports!!!!! Why in heaven's name? Their answer was disarmingly simple. ". . . a month's vacation would give them (the "sportswriters" and all kindred spirits) a chance to catch up on *their* golf, touch football, softball, jogging, bowling, billiards, driveway basketball, hunting, sailing, canoeing, swimming, surfing, fishing . . ."[4] But didn't the editors of Sports Illustrated realize that these are sporting activities, par excellence? Presumably they did since one of their senior editors had informed us that boating, swimming, fishing and bowling were the four most popular participant sports in the U. S. A. (1961).[5]

4. *Sports Illustrated*, 9-8-69, p. 29.
5. Robert H. Boyle, *Sport: Mirror of American Life*. Little, Brown and Co., 1963. Appendix p. 1.

The paradoxical nature of their suggestion, then, is obvious. Let's have a one month moratorium on sport so that we can all engage in the most popular type of sports. This paradox can be solved by the simple substitution of a more precise term. Substitute "highly publicized athletics" for sport and admit that the reason is to get time to play, and the jumbled verbal paradox evaporates. The suggested moratorium pertaining to all those dramatic confrontations of athletes in contests which are sufficiently newsworthy to enjoy newspaper, radio and T. V. coverage. Its purpose was to provide everyone with an opportunity to relax, to enjoy the activity itself, or more precisely, to play.

A second example is far more subtle but can be found in the work of a fellow panelist, Bill Gilbert of *Sports Illustrated.*[6] Gilbert addressed himself to the question of the distinctions which can be made concerning "sport". Examining the hectic history of sport in 1972, Mr. Gilbert concluded that sport exists on at least three different levels. First of all, we have "True Sport," the manifestation of man's seemingly innate urge to play. "True Sport is organized for and often by participants and is essentially a private matter like eating and making love." "High Sport" is True Sport raised to the level of art by the talent, even genius, of its participants. It is public in the sense that all art is public (great music, painting, literature, or sport is incomplete until that time when it is displayed, judged and acclaimed." Finally there is "Big Sport" in which an element of True and High Sport are present but are modified or contaminated by other considerations, notably commerce and politics."

Since Mr. Gilbert may develop this tripartite division of sport in his prepared remarks, I hesitate to discuss his position in greater detail at this time. In passing, however, I cannot resist the following brief observations:

1) I applaud his recognition that "True Sport" is intimately related to play, properly understood, and that it seeks merely to maximize the joy of the activity itself.

2) Since "High Sport" is "True Sport" raised to a level of art by the talent, even the genius of its participants, it would appear that we are concerned with athletes of exceptional ability whose performance attracts the attention of spectators and thus becomes public. It is difficult to see how Mr. Gilbert can consider the dedication and devotion necessary to achieve this high degree of skill as compatible with the playful spirit which he quite properly identifies with the joy, freedom and creativity of play.

6. *Sports Illustrated,* 12-25-72, p. 35.

3) Finally it is most difficult to understand how in "Big Sport" the truly playful spirit can be present at all and to understand what objections Mr. Gilbert can have to the spirit of commerce strongly influencing this type of athletic activity which he rightly designates as a type of entertainment.

I cannot find any truly playful element in Olympic competition or in other so-called amateur contests in which the competitive spirit burns intensely. Here we deal with the great talent or even genius but in no sense a genuine playful spirit.

As a third example, consider the Empire Games of 1954, held in Vancouver, and the bizarre events that surrounded the marathon. I will reproduce, almost verbatim, *Sports Illustrated* account of this dramatic event.[7] Jim Peters was England's champion marathoner. At Vancouver's Empire Games he was winning again. Behind him lay a run of 26 miles — ahead, only a few hundred yards to the official finish. His nearest rival toiled along at least 15 minutes behind. The crowd, still flushed from the fantastic mile of Bannister and Landy, watched expectantly as Peters appeared at the top of the stadium ramp. Then the crowd stiffened.

Peters began to weave and stagger. Grotesquely, like a figure in an impossible fantasy, he fell, rose, fell again. Ten times he fell, only to pull himself up and try for a few more yards.

The crowd shouted encouragement. "Go it, Jim" cried a girl athlete. "That's what made England great." Others tried to halt the heartbreaking wasting of a man. "Stop it, for Heaven's sake," called Roger Bannister, a physician and champion miler. Peters fell across what spectators thought was the finish line and was placed on a stretcher. But as the crowd cheered, a voice rasped over the public address system. "The finish line . . . is on the other side of the track." Peters race was over.

I have no difficulty, according to my definition of athletics, considering this a memorable, if highly controversial, athletic contest. But I find it totally devoid of all spirit of play.

A third example of the failure to make important distinctions can be found in today's intercollegiate football. John McKay has an excellent track record for laying it on the line—telling it as it really is. While most college coaches still cling to the myth that college athletes are collegians in the accepted sense of the word; in other words, that they are students first and athletes second,

7. *Sports Illustrated,* 8-16-54, p. 31.

coach McKay will have no truck with such nonsense. Back in the fall of 1969, when student unrest plagued most campuses and especially the athletic departments, John McKay spoke out on the question of the college athlete. To hold that an athlete is a student first and an athlete second, is according to coach McKay, "the first lie." He went on to explain that when he recruits a boy for U. S. C. he offers him (1) the chance to play on a winning football team, (2) a good education—in that order. He doesn't press the latter because, as he says "a boy can get a good education at almost every accredited school today. But playing football for U.S.C., that isn't something you can do anywhere."[8]

Yet despite such honest iconoclasm, experts who normally tell it as it is, occasionally go soft and lose all touch with reality. In a recent article in *Sports Illustrated* by McKay an unexpected deviation occurs. After explicitly citing Bear Bryant, Bob Devaney, Tommy Prothro, Jonny Majors and Vince Gibson as men who had turned losers into winners and lauding the effects of a winning spirit on campus—"You can feel it build on a campus. All the smiles. Everybody running around saying we're No. 1. Lose 27 in a row and see how many smiles there are"—McKay inexplicably addresses himself to the importance of winning in athletics and then blows the whole thing. Yes, despite his documented and indisputable argument in support of winning, he concludes with an astonishing non-sequitur. "Is it O.K. to play at the top level and lose year after year . . . ? Yes. Winning isn't everything. That's a terrible philosophy to go by . . . It's enough that you play. You desire to win, you try to win, but it's enough to play." Of course winning isn't everything, but it is the primary goal or objective of every athlete worthy of the name. It is literally absurd to say that in big-time college football, it is enough that you play. In fact, the Trojans of Southern California don't, in any meaningful sense of that word, play. They either win with almost monotonous regularity or the crowds dwindle and McKay goes job hunting. If you know the meaning of athletics you know immediately an afortiorti that winning is of prime importance. Moreover, if you know the meaning of athletics and the meaning of play you know immediately that athletes do not play.

The following case history emphasizes the importance of making distinctions.

Some coaches may actually mean it when they say that winning is not their primary concern, that as they view it, *fun* is the

8. *Sports Illustrated,* 9-10-73, p. 32.

name of the game and that playful spirit must predominate at least on the high school level. Their sincerity in this matter can be tested various ways. It is one thing for a high school coach to talk about athletes playing and to sing the praises of the playful spirit, but when winning and fun come into direct confrontation, there are very few coaches who will opt for fun and play.

Consider a concrete case which actually occurred—probably many times. Each year high schools draw up social and athletic calendars and individual events are scheduled months in advance. The senior prom may be scheduled in the fall for the following spring and the same thing is true for the finals of the state baseball championship tournament.

Suppose as was actually the case in the instance we are considering the baseball finals were scheduled for the second Saturday in May with the Senior Prom scheduled for the third Saturday. Spring arrives and as May approaches, many preparations for the big dance have been made. A dance band has been hired, restaurant facilities have been reserved, new gowns purchased and the thoughts of many young girls are on little else but the Prom and its aftermath. But at this point serious complications begin. The baseball finals scheduled for the second Saturday of May bringing together four teams from various parts of the state are washed out by a deluge. Deliberations among the coaches and players reveals that the only appropriate date for re-scheduling will be on the third Saturday of May. But now what about the Senior Prom. The game site is 150 miles from the Prom location and the two games that each team must play to determine the championship will run into the late afternoon with little chance of getting home much before 10:00 p.m.

Now suppose the star pitcher and shortstop on the team which has the Prom scheduled go to the coach and express their regrets, but inform the coach that they won't be able to compete in the championship playoff because of the previous dance commitments. Suppose they argue that they have promised to take their girl friends to the dance and that in light of this promise, the girls have gone to a good deal of work and expense. They feel a moral obligation to keep their promise. Besides, they remind the coach that it was he who told the team that baseball was a fun game, that the important thing was playing—not winning. Since these were his convictions concerning high school baseball how could he possibly object to them pursuing the playful spirit at the dance rather than on the baseball diamond.

For statistical purposes, it is unfortunate that few coaches face such crises, so that we could measure their fidelity to the principle the winning is not important—fun is the thing. But for the peace of the school and community it is probably a very good thing that such crises are rare. Despite their fun and games speel at service clubs and boy scout meetings, I don't believe I ever met a successful high school coach who could act with calmness and equinimity in such a situation. He would rant and rave, charge treacherous disloyalty. Because coaches are among the most competitive of men, he simply couldn't comprehend how a competent athlete would pass up a chance to win a state championship in order to go to a dance.

John McMurtry
Professor of Philosophy
University of Guelph

We tend today to confuse the concepts of sport and athletics. Little or no distinction is made between them. A sports program or an athletics program, a sportsman or an athlete — we use these terms and phrases interchangeably, indifferent to the fundamental opposition of sense which has been with them since the times of the ancients.

The word "athletics" or "athlete" comes from the classical Greek "athleo" which means literally "to contend for prize". Hence the Olympics and professional football, or school competitions and organized kids' hockey leagues — all these are properly called "athletics" and their participants "athletes." For in these and countless other similar cases, the players are pitted against one another in contest, competition, *contention* for an extrinsic benefit, a *prize:* whether the prize in question be a gold medal, a large sum of money, a league trophy, or simply formally recognized victory status.

On the other hand, the word "sport" comes from the ancient Roman "disportare" which means literally to "dis-carry" — that is, to be released from burden, to act for the sake of the activity itself and not for the extrinsic benefit it may yield. To move one's body free of care or "load on one's shoulders" with the movement in question as end-in-self. Hence children's games, pick-up football or shinny hockey at any age, races or contests for the pure fun of it, indeed any physical activity (including love-making) which is not made instrumental to ulterior pay-off — all these are properly called sport.

Thus sport, as I have it here, is by its very nature in exclusive disjunction with athletics. So long as the form of physical activity in question is liberated from ulterior consideration and enacted for the sake of itself alone, it is sport. So soon as it involves ulterior consideration, a prize, for which the participants compete against one another, it ceases to be sport and becomes athletics. The distinction here is clear and intractable, the forms of activity concerned are mutually exclusive. In a word, sport is play and athletics is business.

("Okay boys," goes the near universal admonition of athletics expressing this precise distinction, "Enough play. Let's get down to business".)

II

Most broadly construed, *Contest-for-Prize* (Athletics) and *Activity-for-Itself* (Sport) may be seen as the primal ways of life on earth. The two basic frameworks of all animate motion. Consider, for example, the struggle for survival in nature and history as the athletic form (contest for the prize of life and reproduction). And then consider, on the other hand, the sheer play element in animal and human culture as the sport form (activity disemburdened of extrinsic stakes). I suggest that one may see all animate motion as taking one or other of these contrasting forms, that these are the fundamental modes of bodily movement on our planet.

Written history of course seems almost entirely a matter of the athletic form. Here the more primitive contest for survival and reproduction amongst the fish, fowl and beasts is elaborated by man into endlessly various and subtle patterns of contention for every kind of exclusive prize imaginable: not only the material means of life and sexual mates, but political power, money accumulation, public fame, title, trinket — to name but a few. Indeed it is interesting to note just how explicit the athletic form has been through history. From ancient times where the conquest of Troy by the Greeks seems more or less a championship game between the greatest teams of warrior-athletes the two sides can muster, through the feudal era of lord-led tournament battles, to the contemporary world of Pentagon game-theorists, Presidential game-plans and big-power showdowns, the athletic form in its most literal sense is scarcely concealed. When we observe as well that our traditional institutions of justice are blatantly billed as constituting an "adversary system" (originating in hand-to-hand fighting matches and still formalized as, say, Regina *versus* Jones), that our essential notion of democracy is that there is an official opposition and regular electoral *contests,* that our way of life is almost universally acknowledged as a "race" (albeit of rats) with "winners" and "losers", those who "make it" (i.e., society's top team) and those who don't, and so on and so on, it is really quite remarkable that no philosophy or theory of human affairs has ever drawn upon the athletic model as an explanatory tool: an explanatory tool that might well account for man's otherwise inexplicable and insane record of sustained mutual destruction, antagonism and strife since time immemorial. The contest-for-prize framework alone seems to make sense of all this ruinous human intercourse. On other counts, history seems — as so many of our artistic sensibilities have rendered it — a cruel and interminable absurdity.

Unwritten history, on the other hand — where it is not merely further and unrecorded elaboration of the contest-for-prize motif in sibling rivalries, generation conflicts, personality contests, and so on — is more generously disposed towards sport. The unremarked moments of playing with rather than contending against, of engaging in activity for itself rather than extrinsic pay-off have always had a more prominent place in our lives when we are off the embattled historical stage. But I suspect this prominence of sport in our personal lives is diminishing. As youngster's games, adults' leisure and so on are ever more informed with the structures of organized competition both participant (e.g., child hockey leagues) and vicarious (e.g., game-of-the-week spectatorism), sport seems increasingly threatened with extinction. The contest-for-prize framework seems on the verge of becoming the *only* form of human life accessible to us. Our present I fear is bound in the direction of the inexorable universalization of the athletic model, the ever more exhaustive conversion of the human condition into audienced competition for exclusive reward.

III

The following though, at least, may be said against the *athletic form. By structuring activity as a battle for winner spoils* (whether such winner spoils — and this term deserves pause — be in the form of mere recorded final score or money-and-prestige jackpot), it turns participants against one another in action; it removes attention from sheer physical expressiveness and abandon to coming out on top; it causes negative emotions of fear of failure, hostility, and vanity; it raises a costly and authoritarian official superstructure to regulate, grade and command performance; it yields a caste system of winners and losers, big-league and bush-league, small minority of doers and mass majority of watchers; and it generally promotes a value-system of self-interested pursuit, elitism, us-them divisiveness, obedience to authority, and instrumentalization of activity. The athletic, the contest-for-prize framework is, in a phrase, a bad trip. As the ancient Greek word for contest — *agon* — indicates, it involves us in the systematic commitment to human suffering.

Pretty well the only argument *for* the athletic form is that it uniquely develops top quality performance, excellence, upon which our whole achievement of civilization rests. But such an argument, of course, does not apply — or certainly ought not to apply — to *leisure* activity which is such precisely because it does not require high standard performance to support our technologically advanced or "civilized" way of life. To demand that leisure as well as work be governed by the excellence-imperative is simply illicit extension of principle from one area to another which is its opposite: a crude fallacy.

However, I have more fundamental misgivings about the worth of this argument in favour of the contest-for-prize framework. That is, the claim that it specially develops excellence seems to be frontally mistaken aside from all distinctions between work and play. It is *assumed* by us that the competitive form so fosters excellence of performance, but the grounds for this assumption are so far as I can see either silly or non-existent. What the contest-for-prize framework does, as I've already suggested, is to *distract our attention from excellence of performance by rendering it subservient to emerging victorious.* And it is utter confusion to construe excellence and victory — as we conventionally do — as amounting to the same thing. It is the plainest truism that the winner of a contest is not always so by virtue of higher quality performance, but is very often if not generally so by virtue of dirty tricks, spoiling, intimidation, injury, concealed cheating, manipulation of officials and all the other anti-excellence practices so familiar to contest-for-prize contexts. Furthermore, it is one of the most common — if least spoken about — experiences of participants in a contest-for-prize framework that fear of losing vitally inhibits them from the innovation, adventurousness and simple "letting-go" which would otherwise fire them into performances of a far higher order than they in fact manage. So it seems evident from ordinary experience that the athletic form does not specially ensure excellence of performance, but on the contrary strongly militates against it. I suspect that our conventional mistake of presuming the opposite — presuming that the contest-for-prize framework and excellence of performance are somehow related as unique cause and effect — may be the deepest lying prejudice of civilized thought. Rooted perhaps in the very struggle for existence that has hitherto been the lot of life on earth: as present winners of this contest, we must somehow be the best. To maintain this confusion is the price of accepting ourselves.

Let me conclude though on a more specific note. Considering sport and athletics in the more normal narrow sense, as forms of leisure activity, it seems to me that there can be few more important enterprises than reversing the trend from sport (physical activity for itself) to athletics (physical contest for prize). To do such must not only alter the nature of our free time, but must because of the enormous influence the sport or athletic framework exerts on the character-formation of the young and even the not-so-young — it acts in a way as the social paradigm for both — alter the nature of our way of life as a whole. It has the promise of revolutionary change, as our unexamined term *recreation* hints to us. And in the service of such a movement from the athletic to the sport form, I would think that the following radical judgements were required. One, exclusive rewards or prizes of any sort — from mere formal recognition or special privileges to great money rolls — are all foreign impositions on play (systems of competitive pay off belong, if anywhere, to the unenlightened contexts of market-place and war). Two, keeping score in any game — especially team games — is a substantial indication that the activity in question is not interesting enough in itself to those who keep score (They ought to try a different game, or rediscover the one they're playing). Three, all public financial support for sport from any level or agency of government at any time is only properly directed to the preservation and creation of more public play areas — neighbourhood rinks, fields, courts indoors and out and open to all (Public funding, presently enormous, of arenas for elitist hockey-empires, of various palaces for Olympic promotion schemes, and so on is merely disguised big handout to big business). Four, official superstructures of non-playing game rule-makers and rule-enforcers presiding over people's play in pyramids of non-participant power are all of them unnecessary, wasteful and repressive (Their essential function is only to standardize and perpetuate the contest-for-prize framework in the face of participants' spontaneous disposition to play for fun). And, finally for now, the strict separation between work and play is an iron-curtain between the primary forms of human activity that detracts from both, and that could be progressively lifted with the introduction of the true sporting element into our working lives: recreation flowing over from the sphere of leisure to slowly ease us from that long riveting of our job activities to fixed and joyless routine for the extrinsic benefit of private profit alone towards productive expression with others as a pleasure in itself.

In the movement from the athletic to the sport form, we move from the dramatic staging of life to the integral living of it. We re-enter.

Bil Gilbert

Editorial Staff

"Sports Illustrated"

This is the fourth affair of this genus I have been to since January. Three of them were universities, and one oddy enough was sponsored by kind of a consortium of industries, and in all of them the subject was Sports or Athletics or play, or games, or something like this. The subject was in all cases treated with high seriousness. This indicates several things, first of all that we are getting to be a kind of society that has a lot of time to consider our navels I guess, and secondly it means that I have considerable leisure since I attended four of them. I guess I have mixed feelings about it. I have always had the feeling that sports had a far more influential role in human behavior than often times it has been given credit for. On the other hand, I think it is an activity that doesn't lend itself too well to high seriousness.

Twenty years ago we used to sit around worrying about T. S. Eliot in Canada, same vein you know. I haven't heard of T. S. Eliot in years, I guess we can worry him to death, and I think there is a little danger there. You know that we might worry about this thing a bit too much. It's a subject that is important like laughter, but one of the deadliest things in the world is to go to a conference about the meaning of humour. They're terrible. So, I think that one of the reasons for the seminar is that people like the three of us here . . . might not be particularly witty, but we are always wordy. Our profession is to sling words around. Because words lend themselves nicely to it, we tend to all have a great weakness for what I call taxonomy classification. Our problem is that we take the obvious and we can classify it until it is unrecognizable.

There was a fellow named Henry Keises, a Canadian trapper, who pushed westward to the edge of the Rocky Mountains in the 17th century. I like him very much; he is one of my favorite characters in history. He was a poet and not a bad poet for being a fur trapper. He was also the first European who encountered a grizzly bear. Henry met this thing, and he had no idea in God's world what it was. It didn't even look like a bear, but it was obviously a formidable creature. He didn't know what he had for there was no name for it. Nobody could tell him it was a grizzly bear yet. The point I am getting at in my roundabout way is that here was the real thing. Here was a grizzly bear. There was no name or definition, or taxonomical classification. This was not necessary. This formidable creature has properties and powers which are obvious, whether you can classify them or not.

So, now I want to apply this to what we will call sport here. This is like a grizzly bear. It's there — the definition, the classification, and the categories of this thing? It has properties. For example, if you work all day on the assembly line, if you are plumbing or wiring for example, you know you are not involved in sport or play, or athletics, you are doing work. This is a category of activity. It is quite obvious. There is another obvious thing, when you think just a minute about it, "Sport or play has been around for a long, long time." John gave us a little bit of history, and apparently for almost as long as we have known anything about ourselves there have been people who want to play. Why? The reason is that it is a hell of a lot of fun. I think we can make things too complicated. This is a thing that gives pleasure. I think it would be the exception to find anyone in this audience who had not had some fun playing games. We were talking about this last night, and it was a thing that has been working away in my head. When you think about it perhaps the three kinds of human activity which have given us the greatest pleasure, are social activity, sexual intercourse and playing games.

In your life you have a few times when you feel it is great to be you and great to be alive. In my own case I think three of those times they were involved with fun and games. Everything was right, and you felt twelve feet tall. It was a soaring kind of pleasure! I think I was lucky to have it three times, and I think many people have felt some of that.

You play a game of tennis, you play a game of football, you cave, you white water canoe. You say, "I really had a good time, you know, I forgot taxes and I forgot the rest of it. I like this, I want to do it again." It is a damn fool thing, throwing a ball through a hoop, or knocking a ball into a hole or something like that, but it is addictive. You say you know I can put that thing three out of ten times through the hoop, but it would be really nice to be able to do it six times out of ten, and so there is a kind of compulsion to get better at this. It seems to be something worth doing. I don't know why but it strikes me that I have wasted an ungodly number of hours to get better at doing some stupid thing with a ball. In the big broad scope of things it doesn't make a lot of sense, but that desire, compulsion to play, enjoy sport is there. It is strong. It is real whether we define it or not. A person that becomes very good at something moves into the area of art, whether it's painting or musically composing or building.

Then there's the spectator business. We have this very powerful urge to play games. We want sport. Also, we like to watch other people who are very good at playing games. Wherever you have strong human urges the idea of exploiting them occurs to others. This has always been going on. People say, "Ah ha, I can take the playing drive of people, and I can do something in a business way with it," just as you can put the sex drive to work selling cars or magazines. All manner of people have decided they can make a buck from sports.

Obviously, one who makes a buck out of it is the athlete. This is what we hear about most — the fellow who signed a contract for a half-a-million bucks. But, this is peanuts, compared to industries dedicated wholly to making bucks from people's desire to throw a ball through a hoop. We are all part of it, the three of us, we are making our living off the thing, we are parasites on this drive. Most of you here in the audience are hoping to be parasites if everything goes well for you.

Then there are the ones who do it indirectly. There are the people who sell their cars, and sell their cigarettes.

There is still another area where people said, "Ah ha, we take this desire to throw a ball through a hoop and we can do something with it. We can feather our own nest." This is the area which I loosely call power. For example, there is the close relationship between sports and military power. All over the world throughout history, a general or a sergeant, for example, looks at a bunch of people, military people or civilians, and what goes through his mind is: "Here is a bunch who are going to make trouble if I don't do something." So, what is a good way to get them to keep their nose clean? Get them playing games, get them on a field where they are not running around town at night. Where you know they are not bothering church ladies, not breaking up windows. Put the old javelin in their hands. Let them have a game to see who can throw the javelin the farthest. I think this is historically and traditionally a military use of games. There are other people who say wait a minute, the army thinks it works this way, and maybe it will work other places. So we are using sports as a device to promote the maintenance of established organizations in society.

As an example, among other wasted portions of my life, I spent ten or fifteen years coaching a AAU Track Club (a girls track club). Girls track coaches or AAU Clubs are always broke, and they are always hustling for money. We have a device for raising money in which we are using sports. We call it the "broken-window ploy." What this means is, we come around to somebody and say "Unless you give us $100.00 for our track club there is going to be kids breaking windows out. Not our kids, of course, but kids." Now if they are playing games, they won't break windows. Many, many times sports is defended, promoted and funded because deep down there is a belief that if somebody is out there putting those little balls through the hoops, he or she will never break a window. We use sport to promote social stability.

People have also hit upon sport as a device for re-educating people along the lines educators believe desirable. Most of you are probably familiar with H. G. Wells and Konrad Lorenz and their notion that sports sop up our aggressive instincts. It's kind of the old army game about keeping your nose clean. It has always bothered me, because it makes sports a kind of liver of society. That is a place where all the poisons go, and out of these bad things we make a game which is good. It doesn't work that way: What goes in bad, comes out bad.

Another area in which sports is being used for social engineering is the area of women's sports. I think there is no question that in our society we have used this games' playing drive to define the role of women, by denying them the rights to participate equally with men. We say to a woman, "You ought to be feminine." Any woman who has any brains at all is going to hit you on the head if you say, "You ought to be feminine." Because what we mean by feminine is — you ought to be non-competitive, you ought to be non-aggressive, you ought to be an underachiever, and you ought to have a weak sense of self-identity. We have definitely used sports to convince women that these are the attributes that make them desirable.

Alright, so what's so bad about this? You start out with an innate drive. You find ways that you can use it to make money, to make votes, to make for stability, to make women, or to make men, or whatever you want. I don't know really if it's wrong in a moral sense, but I think it confuses us, tends to subvert our pleasure. I think we should be aware of this trend and in our own lives at least resist having our games' playing instinct used for something else.

— 19 —

Discussion Period

Comment from the Floor

Once you no longer have an extrinsic prize, a victory-status, score a bankroll or whatever it is, then you are permitted to get into the activity as a sheer end in itself. This creates a difference — as soon as people start to keep score and there starts to be a league or anything of this ranking. Extrinsic benefits start to govern the situation. Then people start getting antagonistic and bending the rules and start trying to intimidate one another. And once you get away from extrinsic benefit as a controlling goal of activities, you are relaxed, you are free to follow the activity itself, experiencially let alone conceptually. I find the greatest possible difference between thinking of the other person as the opposition; and even if there isn't a score, there is that opposition. One of the ways that we play basketball is just when one team starts scoring a lot more than the other team and you are not keeping score and you notice this is happening you start switching players around.

JAMES KEATING

With regards to competing and excellence the general impression that has been conveyed is that in athletics everyone is forced to compete. This is one aspect of life in which you choose to compete.

While I was a Dean of a small college for five years, we were trying to schedule major teams, Big 10 teams, Notre Dame and so on, and we went out begging. "Will you please play us?" We went out begging to get this type of rebuff. Our idea was that we wanted to play Notre Dame, and we wanted to play Illinois. We sought this voluntarily, and it wasn't a question of using man not as a person, but as a thing. What in effect was involved here, was that it has as much competition as almost anything that I can think of. You go voluntarily, and you ask other people to test their skills against yours. Some claim these fellows are not looking for excellence but they are trying to make the team.

Basically, you can kick it around no matter how you want it, but it is true they are trying to make the team. The way you make the team is to prove to the coach that you are a more superior football player than the other man who is also attempting to get that particular position.

BIL GILBERT

Or you wear shorter hair or you pray oftener.

JAMES KEATING

Now give me an example where that is true.

BIL GILBERT

I am not arguing that this is a common thing, but I am saying that there is a lot of other factors other than excellence that go into making any kind of a team. And you know *obedience,* you know coaches by nature are a conservative group. I have been a coach, you have been a coach, and the thing that startles coaches beyond all else is boatrockers.

Coaches are worse than politicians. This should never be but the coach wants to win above everything else. There are people of less excellence who have not played in a game because they disturb the coach for a political or social or economic reason. Now you know that as well as I do.

JAMES KEATING

If discipline or self-discipline is a dirty word, if you don't particularly like discipline, well then, it is true that you should avoid at least team sports, but you should also avoid things like the Black Panthers, the Weathermen, the Marxist Party, and many other revolutionary groups where discipline is highly regarded. Discipline is one way of achieving an end. In athletics discipline is necessary. To those who don't like discipline, sports is just not your bag. And I have said before that I applaud all the things that have been said in praise of play, but if you want to be an athlete and you are on a team, ball club. That is undoubtedly true.

How long you cut your hair is a matter of discipline. Your social values are a matter of discipline. They are, but this is a different kind of discipline; it has nothing to do with excellence in either sporting or athletic activities.

— 21 —

BIL GILBERT

And, to make a team you often have to. You are disciplined in this way.

JOHN MCMURTRY

I think that the gold medal by no means is not the only extrinsic benefit that goes to amateur athletes. There are just countless species of extrinsic benefits and awards all the way up from winning the competitions to making the team, to getting various advertising payoffs after the event, and on and on. You are winning races all the way through to make the team, and that extrinsic benefit is commanding your performance all the way, let alone the Olympic gold medal. It is an exclusive benefit granted to you and not to other participants, and that governs your activity whether it's a gold medal or not. You may be satisfied that you are not going to make the gold medal, but you are going to make the free trip and all sorts of VIP treatment, social status and publicly recognized and on and on. You're interested in it and you're going for it, and I have never seen an amateur athlete who didn't behave in this way.

"WHY OLYMPICS?"

William McNichols
Mayor
City of Denver, Colorado

James Worrall
Canadian Representative
International Olympic Committee

Roger Rousseau
Commissioner General
Olympic Games — 1976

Chalmers Hixson (Chairman)
Director, School of Physical Education
Wayne State University

William McNichols
Mayor
City of Denver, Colorado

It has been said, and I think correctly, that the Olympic Games serve as a microcosm for the youth of the world. While the games are structured around athletic competition, their function transcends physical endeavor and reaches into the total concept of living. When the twenty-first modern Olympiad opens in your great nation in 1976, it will actually represent the 315th recorded Olympic Games. The Olympic pageant of sports, which started with a single foot race, is known to cover approximately 3000 years.

Modern man has devised a number of vehicles aimed at promotion of a better understanding among nations and people. None possesses the potential for impact among the youth of the world as does the Olympic movement. If we are to approach achievement of our dreams of world fellowship in the future I submit the primary thrust must be in the direction of the young — for it is here the key to the future rests.

From the earliest beginning, if we are to accept the written works of historians, the Olympic Games were conducted on the highest plane — almost a religious one. For centuries moral standards were carefully upheld.

The mechanics of this athletic festival were developed down through the years. It has been written about these earliest Games, "The world looked to peace and cooperation — and good will to man — through the Olympic Games."

By their very nature the Olympic Games were subject to human interpretation which resulted in something short of perfection. The spirit behind the ancient Olympics was basically one of amateurism and yet, because of the human element there developed flaws and misunderstandings which eventually led to the suspension of the Games in 394 A.D. As long as the high moral and religious nature of the participants and officials continued, the Games were both successful and popular. When morals slipped and the Olympic spirit became clouded, a suspension which lasted 1300 years was the result.

This does not mean the Olympic spirit was wrong, but rather man's imperfection diminished their effectiveness as a vehicle for universal understanding.

Baron de Coubertin successfully revived the spirit and glory of the Olympic Games in 1892 after two earlier unsuccessful attempts by the Greeks by returning them to their earlier concept. Despite the human frailties which clouded the Munich games last year, the Olympic spirit lives today.

I have been asked to address the question "Why Olympics?" today. This is a subject with which I have had considerable experience in recent years.

In 1963 a small group of Coloradans conceived the idea of bidding for the 1976 Winter Olympic Games. They took their idea to the Governor of Colorado, who agreed that great benefits could accrue to the citizens of our state, especially its younger citizens, if we could achieve the honor of hosting a Winter Olympiad.

The Governor appointed a Colorado Olympic Commission, to which the state legislature appropriated funds on a unanimous vote. In nine subsequent resolutions and bills between 1966 and 1972 the Colorado General Assembly endorsed the Olympic effort and appropriated funds. Most of these votes were unanimous.

In 1967, the Colorado Olympic Commission requested that the City of Denver make the bid for the 1976 Winter Games in accordance with the Olympic rules. There was a great wave of enthusiasm across the state and in the City of Denver. Denver City Council passed a resolution endorsing the Olympic proposal and appropriated funds for the preparation of an invitation to the United States Olympic Committee.

In December of that year the USOC chose Denver as the United States city to make the 1976 Winter Olympic bid and there was great joy.

When I became mayor of the city of Denver one year later, six years of hard work on the part of hundreds of citizens and officials had been contributed to the Olympic effort.

During this period — and up until late 1972, nine separate and unanimous actions by city council had endorsed the Olympic effort.

Prior to our invitation team leaving for Amsterdam in May of 1970 we were further bolstered by a unanimous Senate-House resolution by the United States Congress endorsing the Denver bid for the Olympics.

Joy was paramount when Denver was selected by the International Olympic Committee to host the 1976 Winter Games. Not one voice in opposition was heard.

I felt then, as I do now, that no greater opportunity or challenge could be afforded any city than to host the Olympic Games.

As a relative newcomer to the Olympic proposition I had not personally been exposed to the Olympic experience. I had that opportunity at Sapporo, Japan in February of 1972 and again in Munich in September of the same year. These two experiences brought home to me the real meaning of the Olympic spirit and concrete answers to the subject to which I have been directed today.

I endorsed the 1976 Denver Winter Olympics, and I worked to make them a reality. Although I felt great personal disappointment at their demise, I knew that as an elected official I must accept the mandate of the voters and move to other issues.

I remain convinced that the Olympic Games offer an unparalleled vehicle for the good of mankind. I doubt very seriously that there is anything to compare with that feeling which comes when you stand in the middle of an Olympic athletes' village after the day's competition is completed and watch the youth of many nations engage in an exchange of pins, mementoes, and friendship.

As I said earlier, the imperfections of man do indeed sometimes rise into view at the Olympics. This is sometimes evident in the competition — and it was evident for the world to see on television throughout that tragic September 5, 1973, at Munich. I ask if you can completely eliminate the human element from any endeavor in which people are involved, and I subscribe the answer must be negative.

Why Olympics?

I believe you can divide those benefits to be reaped from the Olympic Games into two categories: the human and the physical.

A host city reaps the benefit of both, the world reaps the benefits of the human element.

Avery Brundage outlined in March of 1967 the rationale of Baron de Coubertin when he led the Olympic revival in 1896: "De Coubertin did not revive the games merely to give contestants an opportunity to win medals and to break records, nor to entertain the public, nor to provide the contestants a stepping-stone to a career in the business of professional sport, and certainly not to demonstrate the superiority of one political system over another."

His thoughts were that the Olympic Games would: "Bring to the attention of the world the fact that a national program of physical training and competitive sport will not only develop stronger and healthier boys and girls but also — and perhaps more important — will make happier and better citizens through the character building that follows participation in properly administered amateur sport, also — demonstrate the principles of fair play and good sportsmanship, which could be adopted with great advantage in many other spheres of activity. Participants in the Olympic Games are the youth, and so the future of the world. The value of winning by the rules, ever mindful of sportsmanship and fair play is a lesson learned on the field of sport which can prepare our youth for later success in their chosen endeavor. Hundreds of thousands of our outstanding young people learn true dedication to personal goals as they strive for Olympic participation. Those hundreds from each nation who prevail in the final analysis and become members of Olympic teams are living proof of what it takes to be a winner — and the lessons are adaptable to more fruitful and satisfying living by the rules and winning through dedication to the goal."

The third aim of De Coubertin's plan would stimulate interest in the fine arts through exhibitions and demonstrations and thus contribute to a broader and more well-rounded life.

The arts are a very integral part of the Olympiad. I shall never forget the pageant which preceded the Sapporo Olympics — a revue of Japanese culture, music, and dancing conducted — for the most part — by the children of Sapporo. This was their opportunity to show visitors from around the world their culture, their music — and their philosophy of life. I cannot imagine anyone who had the opportunity to see this event in the large hall — or on national television — who would not be deeply moved by it.

In Sapporo — and in Munich — the great concert orchestras who performed the classics, the traditional small groups who performed folk music and dancing — the exhibitions of art works — all were an integral part of the festival — and all added to the spirit of international understanding and friendship.

De Coubertin felt the Olympics would teach that sport is play, for fun and enjoyment and not to make money and with devotion to the task at hand, the reward will take care of itself.

The Olympics would create international amity and goodwill, thus leading to a happier and more peaceful world.

At Olympic time more than any other the heads of state, municipal officials, state or provincial officials, and the people of all nations come together in a festival of friendship.

The athletic competition and cultural exchange provide the rationale, but the central theme is one of people understanding people. To witness the breaking down of language and cultural barriers is an enlightening and refreshing experience.

I am reminded of the lasting friendships which were made by most of my fellow Denverites who had the privilege of watching the 1972 Olympiad and participating in the non-athletic events.

This, to me, is what the Olympics are all about. Despite some of the well publicized areas of friction and the tragedy of Munich — which could have happened anywhere — the Olympics as a vehicle for understanding and goodwill are unparalleled.

James Worrall
Canadian Representative
International Olympic Committee

Just recently in Varna, Bulgaria, the International Olympic Committee met with officials of the international sports federations and the national Olympic committees in an Olympic Congress.

The objectives of this meeting were to obtain the views of the sports federations and the national Olympic committees on the various problems that face the Olympic movement and the Olympic Games.

The last previous Olympic Congress took place in 1930.

This does not mean that the International Olympic Committee had not had the benefit of the views of national Olympic committees or sports federations over the years between 1930 and 1973. The IOC has heard from them all, along with massive quantities of advice from the media.

However, meeting together provides an opportunity for all to hear each other's views, discuss the various suggestions and the various complaints.

The International Olympic Committee comes under a great deal of criticism, as do the Games and the concept of Olympism. This is particularly true in the last few years with the astounding growth of the Games.

Obviously something is wrong.

On the other hand, the Olympic movement is now officially represented in more than 130 countries and some 900 million viewers around the world were reported to have watched the 1972 Olympics in Munich.

Equally obvious, then, something must still be very much right in the Olympics and the Olympic movement.

A survey of the criticism of the Olympics indicates that most of the concern revolves around six aspects.

The Eligibility Rules, the increasing size of the Games, the soaring costs of staging them, the commercialism that surrounds the Games and the politics and political objectives that intrude upon the event. After Munich, there is the obvious concern of violence and terror.

These problems are very real, highly visible, and extra- ordinarily complex.

The Eligibility Rules endeavour to distinguish between professional sport and amateur sport. To most people, including many within the Olympic movement, this distinction is viewed as one between athletes who compete for wages, and athletes who compete for the love of the sport. This distinction is, however, hazy at best. A professional athlete loves his sport and an Olympian medallist, in many cases, can anticipate rewards deferred until after he steps out of the arena.

It would seem easy to say — "stop all the nonsense and let each country send its best athletes — amateur or professional". But the moment this apparently logical decision is made, the IOC accepts the concept that the Games are not for athletes, but for countries in competition.

On the other hand, it is easy to see that there is already a very strong element of country versus country, with the media producing the medal and point count hour by hour.

If, however, the IOC says — let the Olympics be country versus country, the games will cease to serve the interests of Olympism in the sports development in most of the countries in the movement. The IOC would be staging an event where a few super-powers competed for an accumulation of points. The majority of countries would not send teams, and the concept of the games would disappear.

The problems of scale — too many events, and too many athletes in each event — is another serious problem.

The larger countries, with greater sports development programs, send three athletes for each event — "cut them back to two or one", say the critics. But here again, a subtle change in the concept of the Games is probable. If Country X, with 2 million population and Country Y with 200 million, can each send one athlete for each event, it would reduce the size of the Games and make the competition between countries more even.

But Olympism is not concerned with country versus country. It is concerned with athletes meeting in competition and returning home to spread the story of Olympism. Do we want fewer ambassadors in the U.S., where sport is such a strong factor in American life? Is one sprinter in the U.S. as capable of reaching his countrymen as one sprinter from Jamaica reaching his compatriots with the experience and story of Olympic participation?

The point I wish to make is *not* that changes can't be made, or shouldn't be made. The point is that simple answers do not always meet the real needs of the Olympic movement. An obvious answer may, in fact, be the change that kills the concept and converts the Games to a sport spectacular only, rather than a symbol of Olympism.

But then there are critics who claim that Olympism is a dead issue anyway — an anachronism that the world has long since passed by.

What, then, is Olympism? What are the IOC and some 132 national Olympic committees trying to perpetuate?

According to the founder of the modern Olympic movement, Pierre de Coubertin, "the aims of the Olympic movement are to promote the development of those fine physical and moral qualities which are the basis of amateur sport, and to bring together the athletes of the world in a great quadrennial festival of sports, thereby creating international respect and goodwill, and thus helping to construct a better and more peaceful world."

Avery Brundage reviewed the concept of de Coubertin this way, referring to the source of the Games in ancient Greece. "In that ancient era, culture was both physical and mental. It was a harmonious, balanced, well-rounded development of both mind and body that was sought in the contests; beauty and grace, intangible things, were esteemed as well as strength, speed and agility. Honour was held above all. The events were staged in a beautiful natural park. The charm of the Greek landscape was enhanced by the creations of the most accomplished athletes. The finest sculpture in the world adorned the grounds. Music and poetry greeted the ears of the athletes, elegance and good taste surrounded them."

There are two aspects to these two quotations that are fundamental to the problems facing the IOC today. The first is the idealism of the concept. The second is the basic premise that physical and moral qualities are inherent in amateur sport.

The wording of de Coubertin is often taken to imply that physical and moral qualities are lacking in professional sport — and hence professional sport should be shunned as an anathema in the Olympics.

I suggest that this interpretation is wrong. De Coubertin was concerned about amateur sport because he had understood what was happening — that amateur sport had become international and democratic, suited to the ideas and needs of the present, and to the Olympic theme of the whole man.

There was a difference between amateur and professional sport, but it was not in terms of physical development or morality. The difference was in the fact that professional sport was sport staged for the entertainment of spectators, and profit of promoters. Amateur sport was for the fun of participation and profit was irrelevant.

De Coubertin was not interested in displaying a contingent of highly trained, full time athletes, competing in popular spectator events. He was interested in bringing together, through sport, young athletes who were to be doctors, or teachers, social workers or craftsmen, artists or politicians — the young people who were to be an influence in every walk of life in their homelands.

Professional athletes are an influential group of individuals, influential in sport, but also often in other aspects of their society — in appeals for charity, work with the underprivileged, as well as selling cars or shirts or shaving cream.

There is, admittedly, a great change in the world of professional sport between de Coubertin's day and the present. There is, too, an even greater change in amateur sport.

The appeal of the professional athlete is being used for furthering many worthy causes, and the exploitation of professional athletes by promotion is being altered radically to provide a more equitable financial return to the competitors.

On the other hand, amateur sport is becoming more and more an avenue for science, political purpose, and commercial endeavours.

In de Coubertin's day, an athlete practiced his sport in his spare time — and spare time was very limited to most people. Most Olympic sports required little in equipment expense or training facilities.

Today, amateur sport is a subject of research for a wide range of scientific disciplines — and the results are being applied to sports organization and sports performance—sports sociology, psychology, biomechanics, and so on. Sport science has moved from a study role to a basic contributing element of sports society.

The development of equipment, even such basic tools as stop watches, has had a major influence of the costs of competitive participation. In most Olympic sports today, the costs of reaching the necessary standards of competitive excellence are well beyond the means of all but a very few athletes, and even the resources of the sports organizations. In most countries, the state has intervened, directly or indirectly, to provide assistance.

Perhaps even more important is the development of instant communication, and particularly, world wide TV, which has had a profound effect on the Olympics.

Perhaps the problems of the Olympics are not based on such technicalities as Eligibility Rules or numbers of competitors, or scale of operations. Perhaps they lie in the incredible opportunity to spread the story of Olympism via TV — as the world watches the Games.

Perhaps the Olympics can learn from professional sport and lay down some conditions for TV coverage that are part of the price of the TV rights. Perhaps the TV coverage should be governed by a commitment to emphasize the ideals and to reduce or avoid emphasizing country versus country, super-power versus super-power, political system versus political system.

Just as professional hockey is organized to make money, the Olympics use sport to sell a concept — a concept admittedly idealistic — of the whole man, and peace and friendliness among the peoples of the world.

Such a concept may appear an anachronism in this highly commercial world, and in a world polarized into political ideological camps.

But maybe, too, the fuddy-duddy image of an out-of-date, unrealistic and remote IOC is not so far off the track as many seem to think.

Idealism is not dead, or even dying. It is, I suggest, growing, and particularly among the younger generation. Maybe, in fact, the doddering, old fashioned members of the IOC are closer to the modern youth than the generation or two that seems to separate them.

If the IOC is closer to the youth of today than most of us are prepared to recognize, it is also true that the IOC and youth share the problem of a dream — they have a dream, a vision, and a conviction that somewhere in their grasp, is a way to convert it to reality.

Much may have to be altered, much may have to be modified and much may need to be added. For the IOC, the Games have reached a stage of incredible influence and opportunity. The problem is to retain that influence, harness that opportunity, without converting the objective of the Games to a quadrennial sports spectacular staged for entertainment, a political showcase, and economic objectives only.

First and foremost, the Games must be kept for the athletes of the world — those that reach the Games and those that tried to reach them, for those that won medals and those who are today taking up their first test of strength on a corner lot with their playmates along the block.

We know what we want. We know what we have got. We need to know much more about how to put it all together. That is why we held the Congress at Varna — to hear the views, to exchange views with those most directly concerned, the sports federations and the national Olympic committees which have accepted the responsibility of fostering the ideals of Olympism in almost every nation of our modern world.

Roger Rousseau
Commissioner General
The Games of the XXIst Olympiad

Even the most knowledgeable people in the sport world could not be blamed if they do not understand clearly the inner mechanics of the Olympic Games and more specifically the exact duties and responsibilities of their Organizing Committees.

When, to my greatest surprise, I was appointed President and Commissioner General for the Games of the XXIst Olympiad, this is exactly the first question that confronted me.

Yet, at first sight, the privileges and duties of the Organizing Committee, as defined in article 54 of the rules and regulations of the International Olympic Committee, seem quite clear and rather easy to apply.

Article 54 stipulates, and I quote:
"The Organizing Committee entrusted with the management of the Olympic Games must make all the necessary arrangements, subject to the approval of the International Olympic Committee.

"For all the technical arrangements of the Games, the Organizing Committee must consult the International Federations concerned. It must see to it that all the different branches of sport are placed on the same footing and that one is not favoured before another. It is responsible for the integration of the various sports into the program, but it shall meet the wishes of the International Federations as far as local conditions permit. It must at the same time arrange and supervise the cultural program, which forms an essential part of the Games. A full and complete printed report must be prepared for the International Olympic Committee, within two years of the close of the Games.

"Commercial installations and advertising signs shall not be permitted inside the stadium or other sports grounds. Publicity for any Olympic Games should not be released before the conclusion of the preceding Olympic Games."

Article 51, of the same rules and regulations, sheds an important light on the specific duties of the Organizing Committee. According to this article, the organization of the Games is entrusted by the International Olympic Committee to the National Olympic

Committee of the country in which the chosen city is situated. The National Olympic Committee may delegate the duties with which it has been entrusted, to a special Organizing Committee which shall thenceforth correspond directly with the International Olympic Committee. The powers of this Organizing Committee expire at the end of the Games.

However clear are the rules, however well defined are the responsibilities and powers of the Organizing Committee, COJO (which stands for Le Comité Organisateur des Jeux Olympiques) in the case of the 1976 Olympics, the fact remains that the overall mandate of any Organizing Committee is quite complex. When you study closely, as we have done, the various organizations of the past, you soon realize that this general mandate varies quite extensively from host city to host city and from one Olympiad to the other.

This is due to many factors. In organizing the Olympic Games, each host city or country may set different objectives. At the outset, one country may want to project across the whole world its cultural inheritance and image. One other country may wish, on the occasion of the Olympic Games, to promote indirectly its tourist industry. Another country may want to improve its international trade. It must be clearly understood here that these objectives must not be considered in bad taste or contrary to the non commercialization principle of the Olympic Movement; they are a part of the economic impact on any country organizing the Olympic Games. In that context, every host country in the past has always fully respected the principles and the rules of the Olympic Movement.

It is obvious, therefore, that the secondary duties of the Organizing Committee will be different from one Olympiad to the other. The cultural, social and economic make-up of the host country will alter the duties and overall mandate of the Organizing Committee.

In Europe, where the Games were first held in Ancient Greece, and then revived in 1896 by Baron Pierre de Coubertin, it is quite understandable that the objectives are different and, therefore, the mandate of the Organizing Committee far less complex than it would be on some other continent.

From 1896 to 1972, 11 out of 16 Olympic Games and 8 Winter Olympics out of 11 were staged in Europe.

The Olympic Games are, therefore, an old established and cherished tradition in the history of the European nations. Furthermore, Europe as a whole was the cradle of amateur sport, and amateur sport is still a way of life and the major interest of the average European who is not, as we are, so keenly interested in professional sport.

In that context, the Organizing Committee of any Olympic Games held in Europe has already a well established market and a most knowledgeable clientele. In other words, any European Organizing Committee does not have to sensitize its own population and the whole European clientele to the meaning and the benefits of the Olympic Games.

Let's take the case of the last Munich Games for example. In Germany, the Olympic Movement has been the object of countless research, essays, and various works. From university scholars to public school pupils, the Olympic Movement has been scrutinized and studied from all possible aspects.

The world famous Carl Diem, the top organizer of the Berlin Games and the founder of the Cologne Institute, has written thousands and thousands of pages on the Olympic Movement and his work is now considered all around the world as the Olympic bible.

It is, furthermore, the German geologists who have excavated, at Germany's expense, the site of the first Olympic Games in Ancient Olympia. Furthermore, Germany has been for a long time and still is one of the best organized countries in the world as far as amateur sport structures are concerned.

It is not a coincidence that my friend and colleague, Herr Willi Daume, who was the President of the Organizing Committee of the Munich Games, is also President of the National Olympic Committee of the Federal Republic of Germany, and also President of the Deutschland Sportsbund, which is somewhat the equivalent of Sports Canada, Sports Ontario and La Confédération des Sports du Québec. Herr Willi Daume's task in Germany, as President of the Organizing Committee was, therefore, quite different than mine in Canada, and again quite different than Senor Pedro Ramirez Vasquez, who was President of the Organizing Committee of the 1968 Mexico Games.

In Mexico, where some of my colleagues and myself will have the pleasure to meet the authorities of the National Olympic Committee, this coming weekend, Senor Pedro Ramirez Vasquez and his staff had to launch a tremendous national educational program on the Olympic Movement in general and the Olympics in particular, some three years before the Games. As we have done for the last two years in Québec and as we plan to do this year all across Canada, they held various Olympic contests in every public school. Lectures on the Olympic Movement and the Olympic Games were even delivered by world renowned scholars at the University of Mexico.

It is now Senor Vasquez and his colleagues' legitimate pride to have, in such a short time, made the Mexican people quite knowledgeable in Olympic matters. At the opening ceremonies and during the Games, the Mexican people were able to really appreciate and understand the Games.

Between Mexico in Latin America, in 1968, and Munich in Europe, in 1972, stand Montréal and COJO. The organization of the 1976 Olympics confronts us with a unique experience and challenge in the long history of the Olympic Movement. Beside the fact that the Canadian population has to be sensitized to the principles and the philosophy of the Olympic Movement, the challenge is this: 1976 will be the first time, to our knowledge at least, that the Olympic Games are financing themselves through several programmes without direct financial contribution from the different levels of government, and most important without adding to the burden of the host country's tax-payers.

To our knowledge again, no other Organizing Committee had to face such a situation.

In the past, the Organizing Committees of the different Games, whether they were held in Munich, Mexico, Tokyo or Rome, had the full financial backing of their respective governments, and had only to worry about the organization itself.

In other words, they could concentrate all their efforts on solving the numerous and complex problems involved in staging the Olympic Games and not diffuse their energies on financial problems.

This is not our case. And this is not, as it may seem, a bad situation in itself. It is obvious that our obligation to finance the Games ourselves is an additional burden to us, a burden that no one had to assume in the past.

The organization of all Olympic Games is so complex an undertaking and so large an endeavour that any additional responsibility makes it seem an impossible task. But we do not think so. This new situation presents us, I repeat, with a tremendous but inspiring challenge and we are quite confident that with your help we shall carry it with success to its final conclusion.

Our fund raising programmes, as you know, have been launched. Since July 27, the date Bill C-196 was enacted by Parliament, COJO has been working closely with the Postmaster General and his Department to start the coin and stamp programmes. The Honourable André Ouellet launched the coin program in Montréal on September 19. On the very next day, I accompanied him to Calgary to launch the stamp programme at the convention of the British American Philatelic Association.

The Olympic Lottery of Canada Corporation has been formed. Just two weeks ago, the Olympic Lottery was launched at a press conference where it was announced that the tickets for the first one million dollar price will go on sale at the beginning of December, and the first drawing will be held on April 15, 1974.

The success of these self-financing programmes could be a turning point in the history of the Olympic Games. It would be our greatest pride and it is our fondest hope that these programmes will allow any country of the world to organize the Olympic Games in the future.

If these programmes allow the Games, as we believe they will, to be held in Africa, Asia or South America, then we would feel in Canada that the 1976 Olympics contributed in a modest way to propel the Olympic Movement in a new era. We would also feel, at COJO, that the additional task to finance the Games that way will have been not only worthwhile, but most decisive in shaping a new philosophy in the Olympic world.

As you can see, the specific duties of COJO and its general mandate are quite unique and complex. Contrary to what is often believed, it is not up to the Organzing Committee to train the athletes and prepare them adequately for the Games. This is the responsibility of the different national Olympic Committees, and the different Sports Governing bodies, Federations and Associations at the municipal, provincial, national and world levels. In other words, the Organizing Committee sets the stage and the various sports governing prepare the actors.

Yet, in spite of what has just been said, my colleagues at COJO and myself cannot, and must not limit ourselves to the role of stage managers. Even if our role and mandate are short lived as organizers, we are still an integral part of the whole Olympic Movement and we must, therefore, assume the responsibilities it entails. We cannot and must not remain indifferent to the principles and philosophy of the Movement. Alongside with the authorities of the International Olympic Committee, of the 131 National Olympic Committees, of the International Sports Federations, alongside with the millions and millions of people involved in amateur sport and in the Olympic Games, we can and we must meditate on certain basic questions and organize the Games in the light of their answers.

In this respect, the Games of Ancient Greece provide us with a lesson. The enclosure reserved for the Games in Ancient Olympia was almost primitive in character: a paved rectangle, nothing else, no stands, no presidential box, nothing. No fancy or complicated scaffolding to accommodate the judges. The spectators, historians would set their number at some forty thousand, simply took places on the soft encircling slopes which provide natural seating facilities around the stadium. A stone bench was provided for the contest judges only, while officials, high priests and even kings mingled freely with the crowd, under the eye of Zeus who, as legend would have it, watched the Games from atop Mount Cronion.

The Greeks could easily have built a colossal stadium supported by gigantic columns; the Acropolis and so many Greek temples are evidence enough of their skill. However, such a monument erected to their personal glory would have been in their eyes a betrayal of the spirit, the ideal and the very object of the Games which are to ennoble Man and not matter. Even before the coming of Christianity, these Games proclaimed that Man was a god-like reflection, and his whole life on earth but a step on the road to perfection. While in his poems Pindar sings the glory of the victors, he praises more highly still those virtues which make them akin to the gods of Olympia. In other words, the Games of Antiquity stressed the dignity, even the divinity of Man. Can as much be said of the Modern Games?

One thing is certain: many aspects of today's Games do not correspond to the concept of Baron Pierre de Coubertin who revived them. True it was de Coubertin's wish that the Games be adapted to contemporary customs while, at the same time, remaining faithful to their original inspiration. He yearned for Games opposing individuals and not countries. While his Citius-Altius-Fortius most certainly applied to the importance and the quality of performance, it was meant to apply more specifically to the valour of the opponents and the nobility of their encounter.

A teacher by calling, de Coubertin believed that sports practised individually furthered education, and practised collectively developed closer links between nations.

Perhaps it was inevitable for the Games, because of their own dynamics, to suffer, so to speak, from their own success and be entrapped by their very expansion. Perhaps it was inevitable also that the rivalry of the athletes be matched by that of the organizers. What can be more normal, more understandable, more human than for a nation, a state to wish to do as well and in fact better than its predecessors! It would indeed be both false and unfair to look for dark and evil designs in such perfectly legitimate aspirations. However, one would lack realism in denying that from Olympiad to Olympiad the Games are becoming ever more costly, the stadiums ever larger, the organization ever more extensive, the mechanics involved ever more complicated.

This is why, in our capacity as organizers, we must go back to some fundamental values. Namely, as I have said before, that through our self-financing programmes, adapted to the circumstances, every country's dream to host the Games could become a reality. It is only this way that the Olympic Movement will be really felt and understood on the five continents, symbolized by the five entwined circles of the Olympic flag. It is only this way that every athlete in the world will really be involved in the Movement and his efforts rewarded.

It was de Coubertin's dream and it is the Movement's basic philosophy that everybody could take part in the Olympic Games. It was also de Coubertin's deep belief that the athlete should be the focus point of the Games. This is what he called the democracy of sport. This will be possible only if the Games, in the future, are within the financial reach of any nation of the world.

But most important of all, de Coubertin believed that the grandeur and dignity of Man lies essentially in his never ending determination to push as far back as he can the limits of what is deemed impossible. It is in this will to outdo, to master and to purify himself and to soar towards the stars which makes Man akin to the gods.

This was the message of the Greek philosophy. This was also the message of Christianity. But as Blaise Pascal noted, beast lies ever closer to angel, when the effort becomes too demanding and the equilibrium is disrupted between body and mind, between the end and the means of achieving it.

The Greek ideal, made immortal by Socrates and Plato, sung by Pindar, revived by de Coubertin, was a hymn to proportion, harmony, moderation in everything. The Ancient Greeks had a word for this philosophy: eurythmy — an athlete's body, a poet-philosopher's mind.

In simpler terms, the perfect harmony between man's physical capabilities and his intellectual faculties.

Discussion Period

James Worrall

In expressing a very personal opinion to justify the continuation of the Olympic Games in Montreal and in 1980, trusting the world still to be more-or-less at peace, I don't think one can stop efforts in any field of activity, to wait for the world to become perfect. You might as well say that we should have no international conferences of any kind, no international conference in the arts, no exchanges of university students.

Some Canadian students might go to a country where they might pick up some bad ideas. To my mind, this is absolutely untenable and, therefore, I feel very sincerely and strongly that the Olympic movement shall be continued.

Roger Rousseau

I think that I would like to add that I have been in this movement for a year-and-a-half and have been surprised at what it has done for the world. I compare it in the sports world to the United Nations in the political world. I could not really see the world without the United Nations, and I find it difficult to see the sports world without the Olympic Games.

Question

The mechanism of putting on the Olympics shouldn't be in a locked situation, so that anything is countenanced in the games. Is that the thrust of the question? More in this area? And what, for instance, is being done to update the people responsible for awarding the Games as some things happen in the Games, that all of us know, are not condonable? Is there an ongoing process to get this done? I think you indicate that there is.

Roger Rousseau

Well, yes, I have to reiterate. I think there is. I think the organization of the Olympic Movement through the International Olympic Committee, the National Olympic Committee's of one-hundred-and-thirty countries and some twenty-eight international federations is certainly viable.

"TOO MUCH SPORT TO BE BUSINESS OR TOO MUCH BUSINESS TO BE SPORT?"

Donald Canham
> *Athletic Director*
> University of Michigan

Abigail Hoffman
> *Canadian Track Star*
> Department of Political Studies
> University of Guelph

Alan Eagleson
> *Player Representative*
> *for the N.H.L.*

> **Al Ackerman (Chairman)**
> *Sports Editor*
> American Broadcasting Company

Donald Canham
Athletic Director
University of Michigan

I was in Kansas City this morning and TWA went on strike. It took me two-and-a-half hours to get on a Braniff plane. I picked up my car at the airport, and it knocked out about two miles before I got to the Ambassador Bridge, and I had to hitch hike a ride in and I don't know where my car is now. So, I am very happy to be here!

What I thought I would do is just take a few moments to throw out some thoughts because I think the thing that would be of most benefit would be a panel discussion. So, I will not be long. But, I did want to point out a few things that I think you might not have considered.

First of all, I don't think that we are becoming a nation of spectators, or a world of spectators. Although we are now drawing more spectators both in the actual arenas and in television, without any question far more youngsters and adults are competing in athletics and sports than ever before. In the United States, for instance, indoor tennis clubs are springing up all over the country. Indoor ice arenas, as well, are springing up all over the country. As I walk into elementary schools I see gymnasiums that I would have loved to have played in when I was a kid, and I think you are seeing the big business of athletics, benefiting the youth of today. There are more golf courses today than ever before. I think you all realize what has happened to tennis just because of Billy Jean King and the Bobby Riggs match. You couldn't buy a tennis racket after the Astrodome exhibition.

If that is true, what can be wrong with the big business of athletics? I include intercollegiate business as well.

Let me give you an example of what happens at the University of Michigan and most of the major institutions in the United States. The budget from my department, and I am the Director of Physical Education, Campus Recreation, Women's Physical Education, Men's Physical Education, and athletics is three-and-a-half million dollars. We don't submit a budget to the university and say here is what it is going to take us to operate as does the law school and literary college. We submit a budget and then we go out and earn it. We are criticized in Ann Arbor, by some, for hocking our product like it's a trip to the Caribbean. We do. We send out two million pieces of direct mail a year to sell our hockey tickets and our basketball tickets and our football tickets. The reason being, if we don't earn at the gate that three-and-a-half million dollars, we don't have a club sport program in Ann Arbor. We don't have a track team. We don't have a swimming program in Ann Arbor. We don't have a wrestling team. We don't have a baseball team. We don't give three hundred thousand dollars to the intramural program. We don't let the girls play field hockey in the Michigan stadium, because we don't have a Michigan stadium. And, so, from that standpoint athletics is big business. There is no question about it. But, I can't for the life of me, in our particular situation see what is wrong with that.

Now there are an awful lot of things wrong with intercollegiate athletics. There are an awful lot of things wrong with professional athletics. But, I think that most knowledgeable people would have to say that one of the reasons we have this great interest in amateur hockey and amateur wrestling in Michigan for example, is that we have business in athletics that can afford to pay twenty-five million dollars to put the Olympic Games on television. This attracts attention to sports and athletics, and get kids interested when they are young. In addition, the great surge in our country for women's competitive sports is a direct result of the big business of athletics, both professional and amateur.

I think that the Olympic Games televised with Olga Korbut and all those beautiful gymnasts, and all of those wonderful woman swimmers, and the tremendous track athletes that you have seen on the tube have caused the young gals of today to get interested. And, I see nothing wrong with that. I am not going to deny that amateur athletics, at least, in the United States is a gigantic business, because it is. Rather than condemning it, and criticizing it, I would just like you to take a look and see some of the good things that it has done.

Abigail Hoffman
Canadian Track Star
University of Guelph

I am a little confused as is the Chairman about just what the topic of this discussion means. I think what the topic means is that there is a conflict between the aims and objectives and the values of professional and particularly the commercial or commercialized brand of professional athletics, and the world of amateur sport and also the world of play including non-competitive and recreational physical activities.

I understand that you have had a couple of hours in which you tried to straighten out these matters this morning and weren't completely successful. So, I think that I'll take that as a right to be fairly liberal in the use of the terms myself.

I would like to point out some of the pervasive influences of the commercial sport in our sport culture generally. I think that a lot of us here share some concerns and find some of the commercial sports objectionable. Maybe I am putting words in mouths, but certainly this is my own feeling: there are some things wrong with that kind of approach to sport.

I would like to point out ways in which commercial sports interferes or dominates our approach to sport in general.

For example, I can remember being very, very disturbed at the time of the King-Riggs match. What bothered me, bothered a lot of men. I guess we were disturbed by the score, but I was disturbed also by the fact that it was a mediocre display of tennis. Yet, millions of people watched. I watched myself. I got conned into watching this match and sort of indulging in all the related commercial humpraw and I consider myself to be a pretty strong character. I think that does indicate that there is a pervasive influence of a kind in commercial sport. I consider it somewhat objectionable.

I don't think that our main approach to sport is one of a commercial nature. I think that it makes a lot of sense to look at sport as a kind of reflection of the society, the particular society in which it exists. If we look at our own society, a very highly commercialized society, a high consumption, high production, high level of industrialization kind of system, and basically our society is consumer-oriented, we see we're a society that depends on increasing commercial growth, and that depends on all of us here and everybody in the society as increasing demands call for more commodities.

Basically what the big sports promoter or sports entrepreneur hopes as does every other kind of business person, is that people don't have a saturation point in terms of their demand, for what we could call "sports commodities". Basically what the sports entrepreneur hopes for is that baseball, hockey, football, basketball and so on, that these franchises can be extended limitlessly. Deep down we know that the whole society is based on commercial values. Sport is synonymous with the ideas that run the society generally. We kind of have some ideas that society is pretty cutthroat. You can divide people into winners and losers and that most people and many professional athletes can be treated harshly and arbitrarily. Admittedly at $75,000.00 a year it's not that painful to be treated arbitrarily I suppose, but still we are aware that those kind of things do exist in this society and not just in sport, they exist in the society in general.

I think what bothers me and what bothers a lot of us is that we think there should be other values in the society. We tend to look at the sport and say, "Well, after all, sport is merely a leisure-time activity, it shouldn't be a business activity." I think really what the problem is and what the question of this panel is trying to get at is the conflict of values between the commercial sports system and another kind of sport ethos that some of us would like to see prevail, but we know it is kind of an idealistic situation.

I would like to point out a couple of areas where these ideals do clash and the kinds of things that people point to who are critical of the commercialization problem. One thing that has arisen lately in this country is that many can see that professional sports is excessively concerned with the balance sheet of a team or the balance sheet of a league. This has somehow or other diminished quality of play, even at the professional sport level. We look at football and hockey and basketball, and if you look at the length of this schedule, look at the difficulties that players have even keeping themselves in one piece for the duration of an entire season, it is clear on many occasions, that by the time you get to the end of the season, by the time you get to the playoffs the best quality of play has taken place earlier in the season. One reason I like to watch the playoffs in many sports is not because it is the best calibre of play. Very frequently it isn't. It is certainly the most suspense-filled, the most dramatic. Certainly the polarity of winning and losing is most heightened at that time, but it isn't necessarily the best calibre of play. I think that professional commercial sports has done this, because the ideas can extend the season so that baseball season runs into football season, runs into hockey season, into basketball and so on; drama and suspense replace quality and calibre of play and level of excellence. I suppose some people will argue that the calibre of play has in fact increased over the years despite lengthening schedules and those kinds of things. I think that it became fairly clear to a lot of people during the Russia-Canada Hockey series last year. Maybe the calibre of play wasn't in the National Hockey League as it is presently constituted. Maybe it could be, but at the present time, the whole system was mitigated against the best play in a long, long schedule such as that.

One of the other things that disturbs me is the way the media treats the coverage of professional sports. I am not talking so much here about newspaper coverage, but the way in which actual games are portrayed on television. I know there is another whole panel that is going to deal with this, but I did want to say something about this. We have complained and it has been pointed out that professional sport tends to create people who are interested in watching T.V. rather than people who are interested in being active themselves. I know I watch a reasonable amount myself, and I find that I get passive mentally, not just physically. You know you sit down on a Sunday afternoon in front of the T.V. and you are going to watch a football game. You sit there with a kind of glazed, dazed look. You know there is so much technology that tends to repeat everything that is exciting, you know if you miss something there is always the slow motion camera and the stop action camera and the behind the goal camera and the downfield camera, and the upfield camera, plus a couple of experts who are going to tell you every little thing that happened. And, you know you just sort of sit there, not really paying much attention, and then all of a sudden the announcer will shriek out something and you will wake up so you can watch the replay. It is a very artificial sort of thing. I find that watching sports on T.V. as I say is not only physically deadening but it is also very deadening mentally. I find I get a very artificial idea of what the game is all about, that I can't even relate what I see on television to what is actually going on in the field. We should consider too, that, in fact, the largest numbers of spectators are the people who are watching on television as opposed to the people who are watching in the actual stadiums. I think that it is a serious thing that the T.V. professional sports tend to make us a little bit less interested in actually participating and even tend to make us a bit more passive at the psychological level.

One of the other things that we see when we watch T.V. is the complexity of professional sports. There the coaches, incredible technology, the upstairs and the downstairs telephones, every club has got half a dozen coaches or so and medical experts and managers and the whole structure that has to be involved in sports and that is what we see when we watch professional sports on T.V. Again, I think it is a very intimidating experience for many people. People who watch sports on T.V. and who see that kind of thing and see how complex it is find it is a real deterrent. Certainly it can be argued that there is some validity in what Don Canham has said that the sort of business base of sport does create opportunities for more people to take part in sport. But, I think it is worth considering what kind of opportunities they are, and for what people, and what sex and at what ages. If we look at the case of hockey in Canada, and I think most of us are pretty familiar with this, you see hundreds of thousands of kids across the country playing at age nine and ten and as you go up the age rankings there become fewer and fewer players because basically the structure is established so it's ultimately going to let the best players come to the top, because these are our potential professional stars and the rest of the players can fall by the wayside. No one can give all kinds of reasons for that, but I think that it has been amply documented that one of the main reasons is that professional teams are not interested in promoting mass participation. They are interested in promoting the recruitment of players for their own purposes. Maybe that makes sense in terms of their own business interest, but what are the consequences for the senior athletes, for people who are adults. The number of sports opportunities are limited. I don't think that it is too difficult or requires some huge leap to associate that problem with the domination of the commercial sports structure.

Well, the whole status and prestige question always brings up some interesting things if you look at commercial sports. What bothers me is not just the fact that if we read the sports pages we can see that most of the space is devoted to professional hockey, baseball, basketball, football, mostly male sports; but it's the kind of reporting that you get. I so often read, and I think that we all do, about athlete so and so who makes $75,000.00 a year, or some figure in that neighbourhood. In our own minds, I guess because we see that he makes that kind of money, we assume that he must be good. Very rarely do we get the kind of impression that because such and such an athlete is good that he gets this kind of financial remuneration. We tend to be conditioned, to be preoccupied with the financial worth of the players rather than the level of excellence, at which they are performing. Status, prestige, appreciation in sports tends to be connected with the dollar value rather than on the athlete's ability level.

One of the interesting sidelights in terms of the financial aspects of professional sports tending to dominate our sports press is that there is a whole new kind of athletic hero. I can recall in the last year alone leafing through the sports pages of the Toronto newspapers and finding lengthy stories on one of the gentlemen on the panel, on Louis Levesque, on Conn Smythe, on the Molsons', on Bobby Haggard, on the Bassettes, on Gerry Patterson, on Jack Kent Cooke. These are all people who have taken up a lot of space in the sports pages. Where they really belong is, I guess, on the business page. What it means is that not only do amateur athletes in non-competitive physical activities have to compete with professional athletes, for space, for status, for attention, they even have to compete with the sports entrepreneur for attention. I think at that point it may be time to consider that we have carried the business end a little bit too far.

One of the other things that the professional sports tend to do is that they focus on team competition, not exclusively, obviously golf, tennis, and a number of other sports are not team-oriented. And, I think team sports give us a very different approach to athletic participation, and basically what they do is really heighten the winner, loser—polarity. They divide everybody that takes place or part in a game, or takes part in a sport on one day as either a winner or a loser. An example of how professional sports and commercial sport differs from other kind of sports activity can be seen from my personal experience. At the Olympics in Munich, just over a year ago, I finished eighth in the final. Since there were only eight in the final, a little elementary arithmetic will give you some idea what the significance of that is. After I finished, one is confronted by a whole group of newspaper reporters and press people. I tried very hard to explain to these people that I was very happy with my finish, with my place, I had run my best time, a better time than I had ever run before. I felt that I was in the race for the entire time. There is a certain kind of solidarity that is built up among Olympic track and field competitors. In this particular event we were competing on three days, heats, semi-finals, and the final round. We started off with thirty-two people. After the first day sixteen were eliminated, so the remaining sixteen felt a closeness and a bond with each other. Then we ran the semi-finals and eight more were eliminated leaving just eight in the final. I think it is very difficult to convey what that meant. By the third day there was only eight of us remaining out of the thirty-two. We felt much more of a feeling of something in common with each other, than we felt antagonism toward each other. And, yet, it was almost impossible for me to convey this sensation and my pleasure at even having the privilege of running against and running with these competitors in the Olympics. And, I think the reason for that is very simple. Most press men, probably all of them that I talked to there, are people whose idea of post-game activity is more along the lines of the tearful dressing room scene or the drunken celebrations of the winners. This sort of polarization of the winners and losers does exist. Because we tend to be dominated by the professional and commercial sports world the people really aren't aware, as much aware that they could be or I think they should be, of what the alternative approach to sport is.

I guess one reason why I am a little optimistic at least about the future of sports in this country is because the Olympics are going to be held here in 1976. I think there are going to be a lot of Canadians who are going to be introduced to that kind of approach to sport that they wouldn't otherwise see. And, I think that the Olympian approach is an approach that generally speaking the commercial, professional sports don't display.

There is one other aspect that I would like to get into briefly: Women. I just say it bluntly I guess. It's a bit disturbing I think to look through the program and realize that there are only two women who are speaking. I am not about to launch into an attack on the organizers of the conference since they are sitting in some tribulation at the moment. I would like to point out that the sport world tends to be dominated by men, and that, in fact, it may make sense in terms of the amount of interest on the part of women that there is, that women have in sport, that only two women would be on these panels. That is not so extraordinary in itself, but I think that it is worth looking at what professional and commercial sport does to determine the status of women in sports. I am going to do this very, very briefly.

We can see the status of women in the commercial, professional sports field. If you look at any football or basketball game on T.V., one of the most prominent or the only prominent females, generally speaking, are cheerleaders. I happened to see something particularly obnoxious on television. I happened to see a Milwaukee-Buffalo basketball game and there apparently is a new innovation called the "Buckettes". These ladies are rather scantily dressed, which in itself is not objectionable, but their role as far as the game is concerned is objectionable. One of our heroes happens to spit on the floor and one of our Buckettes runs out and sweeps it up. I think it says something demeaning about women. As women are treated in the professional sports structure, similarly are they treated in the rest of society. I think we are all aware of the sort of advertising and the kind of thing which women are used to sell, various kinds of things, but, that is not my main concern. What I am more concerned about is the way in which the rise of commercial sport has limited, and basically had an adverse effect on the possibilities for women to take part in the sport.

Don Canham mentioned that there are more than ever now taking part in sport. I tend to doubt that. In fact, if you look back to the late twenties and the early thirties in this country (and I don't know for sure what the situation is in the states), but in this country there were a lot more women of all ages taking part in sport in the twenties and thirties than there are now. There were some quite amazing things.

In fact, in Toronto all the newspapers had regular columnists, women, who covered women's sports. On the radio, if you can imagine this, there was Terry Blythe. Girls high school inter-school basketball games play by play carried on the radio. You can't even find a score in the newspaper let alone get a play by play description of the games on the radio. And, I think that without going into a long analysis at this point, you can very closely and very clearly associate the rise of commercial sports with its emphasis on the male sports hero as having a very adverse effect on the position of women in sport. I think that what basically has tended to happen is that sports has become not only an acceptable but almost a necessary activity for most young men. It's an activity by which they may ultimately become quite wealthy, or at least it has an occupational possibility for men. It has no comparable occupational role for women except in a very few instances for professional skaters and more recently for golfers and tennis players. Certainly as a major occupation it has a very limited potential for women.

Certainly the sport scene is dominated by the professional teams, and what we are watching for the most part and what we are reading about for the most part is men's sports. Maybe women to a certain extent are to be blamed themselves for not pressing their claims a little harder. I think that is changing very dramatically right now, I certainly hope that it is, but, it is very clear in the post-second world war period our tendency has been to associate sport with men's sport. Even now we can sort of see the vestiges of that if you look in the newspapers and you want to see for example, the listing of results of a high school track meet or various high schools sports. What you generally see are the men's-basketball scores followed by the girls'-basketball scores. This conveys that the really important stuff is the men's games.

As I say I am reasonably optimistic about that kind of thing changing, but certainly I think it would be reasonably fair to attribute some of the problems that women face in sport to the domination of our whole sports culture, by commercial athletics.

Alan Eagleson
Player Representative
for the N.H.L.

Just as my resumé states, I am executive director, manager and executive counsel to the NHLPA, similar confusion reigns in the title. I plan to tell you people about hockey and other major league sports and their direct relationship with business.

Major league sports is big business. More glamorous than most industries, the big leagues are characterized by franchises whose owners and locations change like manufacturing plants, whose dealings are hampered by labour disputes, and whose balance sheets involve millions of dollars. Most sports owners minimize the business aspect of sports because they fear that fans will be averse to supporting a profit-oriented company as the home-town team.

In 1972 alone, more than 60 million North American sports fans spent more than $300 million for tickets to watch 95 major league sports teams run up and down fields or around bases, shoot balls through baskets or pucks into nets.

Television and radio paid $100 million for the rights to cover professional team sports.

Fans spent an estimated $150 million on concessions at the games.

Local, provincial, state and federal governments in one form or another, directly or indirectly subsidized sports operations to the extent of tens of millions of dollars.

These surely are business statements as well as statements of sports.

Sports is a business in almost every sense. The two major exceptions are 1) the ego factor and 2) the reserve clause of employment.

The ego factor can best be exemplified by Charlie O. Finley. Mr. Finley was until 5 or 6 years ago an unknown rich insurance man, making 6 million a year selling insurance policies door to door. Then he decided to buy the Kansas City Athletics (now the Oakland A's), the California Seals of the NHL, and the Memphis Tams of the ABA. In that short time Charlie O. has become the most controversial sports owner in the history of all the leagues he is in. He is recognized everywhere he goes and he loves it. He still makes 5 or 6 or 7 million a year from insurance, but his divisions of Charles O. Finley — (that's what all the cheques say — a division of Charles O. Finley Inc.) lose a couple of million every year.

The reserve clause in every sports employment contract is the other factor inconsistent with general business techniques. In sports, the club owner can trade, sell, or otherwise dispose of his players at his whim, and without any notice. In fact, sports owners would have us believe that they own players from the time of signing, to the grave, although things have changed somewhat now, the Boston Bruins owned the rights to Bobby Orr the day they sponsored a team in Parry Sound, when Bobby was 12. In business if an employee wishes to change jobs and leave Imperial Oil to join Texaco, he is able to do so, providing his contract of employment has expired. This does not apply in sports. Clubs try to prevent any player movement without the club's consent. Only since the birth of the WHA has a hockey player had a choice.

Most other aspects of sports follow business guidelines.

The law of supply and demand is the dominant law today in hockey. There are only so many players available and yet there are 12 WHA and 16 NHL clubs competing for their services. The same applies in the NBA and ABA. As a result, the average salary of hockey players has increased from about $30,000. in 1971 to $55,000. in 1973. In basketball, since the ABA-NBA war started, salaries have gone from an average of $12,000. to $85,000. Contrast these with the average NFL salary which, since the NFL and AFL merged has dropped from $40,000. to $30,000. The demand on talent by the WHA is the main reason for the salary explosion in hockey.

Another major similarity to business is the depreciation of the team assets by the owners. The assets include, of course, the players. The player has such a short career generally that an owner can write off his value quickly, normally over a 5 year or 7 year period. The impact is dual in nature. First it reduces the tax a profitable team would have to pay or second, as in the case of Charlie Finley I described earlier, the owner can apply any loss against his personal income and thus reduce personal income taxes.

For example, in 1962 a Chicago group bought the then Milwaukee Braves for $6.2 million from Lou Perini. They established a player value of $6,168.00, and secured IRS approval to depreciate that amount over 10 years. In the past 5 years the Braves, now in Atlanta, have reported total net income of more than $1.8 million, but that is after legally and properly deducting a paper loss for player depreciation during that time of more than $3.1 million. Net cash income for the Braves exceeded cash expenditures by about $5 million for an average cash flow profit of $1 million per year. As an example, Hank Aaron was an asset when the club was bought in 1962, and here 11 years later he's one of the most important assets in sports, although he has been fully depreciated.

Another similarity to business is the movement of public companies and conglomerates into sports. The most recent example is the Storer Broadcasting purchase of the Boston Bruins from the Adams family. The purchase was approved by the S.E.C. as a tax-free exchange of shares, but let's look at the figures and show you how a good deal became a bad one for Boston shareholders. The merger was announced when Storer was selling for $45. per share with 1.6 shares of Storer for 1 share of Boston. When the deal finally closed Storer was selling for $20. per share. The Bruins at $70. a share were a good buy and at $31. a share were an outright steal. The Bruins changed hands for a cash value on closing of about 5 million dollars even though they had 4 million cash in the bank, a profit of 1 million a year guaranteed, and one asset alone worth 6 million dollars, namely Bobby Orr. I knew I should have bought that team. Oh well, at least that 6 million dollar asset and I get along well, and someday maybe the NHL will give us a franchise just to keep him in the NHL. If they don't, I know the WHA will.

Another similarity is the entry into sports by unions. Of course, since I am President of the Ontario Progressive Conservative Party, we tell everyone it is an Association. It is a union in everything except name and except for the fact that we do not bargain for salaries as a union does. We work on fringe benefits and minimum salaries and other group problems. The rise of the militant player associations in sports is the result of an awareness by the player that sports is a business. They see how they were exploited over the years by unscrupulous owners and feel justified in what some suggest to-day is exploitation by owners of players. There is great concern today on this point in the mind of the public.

I am often asked "Surely Wilt Chamberlain isn't worth $600,000. a year?" I answer, he must be because someone is paying him that amount. The pendulum was on the owners' side of centre for 50 years and there was no public concern. It has been on the players' side for only 2 years and already the public complaint is apparent. It is obvious the owners are great lobbyists and public relations experts.

Let's see if the owners' tears are justified in hockey.

An investment in an NHL franchise in 1967 would have been an excellent one at a price of $2 million. Within 3 years, Vancouver and Buffalo paid $6 million for a similar franchise and a similar price prevailed when Atlanta, Long Island, Washington and Kansas City were accepted as league members.

One of the best examples of a great investment is the Vancouver Canucks. An American company, Medicor Inc. bought the franchise for the equivalent of $1 down, the balance when you catch me. It then set up a company named Northwest Sports, went to the public with an offering and wound up with a franchise fully paid up. Mr. Scallen apparently played some games with some funds and is awaiting the hearings of his appeal from a 4 year jail sentence. Now he wants to sell his 60% of the team for about $10 million. This would put the franchise at a value of about $16 million. Not a bad deal for nothing down and nothing a week for the rest of your life, the Canucks team profit is still about $1 million per year and is one of the most successful hockey franchises.

Another example of sports business attitudes is the reaction to competition. In 1967, when we formed the Players' Association we asked the owners to review the reserve clause. The most they would do was to agree to set up a study committee. That committee met once in 4 years. Suddenly the WHA entered the hockey business. The results were amazing. The owners wanted monthly meetings of the committee even though they had previously had no inclination towards them at all. There is no question in my mind that there will be a removal of the lifetime reserve clause. In fact, it probably doesn't exist now. The cases in the U.S. relating to Sanderson, Hull and the others has shown a player is free at the end of the contract. There is even a suggestion that the inclusion of such a "lifetime reserve clause" in a standard contract makes the contract illegal. Wouldn't the Boston Bruins love to hear that??

The Players' Association is acting on advice from anti-trust counsel on the reserve clause matter. Although we had planned to continue our negotiations with the owners, we have been instructed not to do so. There is a possibility that such discussions might constitute a breach of anti-trust laws in the U.S.

The anti-trust area itself shows a difference exists among sports. In baseball, the Curt Flood decision said baseball is still exempt from anti-trust. In football, Congress approved the NFL-AFL merger and exempted it from anti-trust. The obvious result of that merger was more money for owners and less for players.

In basketball, Congress refused to permit an ABA-NBA merger and the result is more for players, less for owners. We, of course, as an association in hockey must fight any NHL-WHA merger because such a merger can only hurt the players.

So gentlemen, when you read the comments of owners that the salaries of players are becoming ridiculous, remind yourself that sports profits for owners are an important factor in their decision to stay in the business of sports.

Discussion Period

Question

How do men like yourself who are in high-powered negotiations with television networks who are trying to fill up stadiums, worried about the downfall of the Big 10, justify the human values we are talking about in regards to young athletes? And, the fact that this has to be a money-making proposition, or by God, the University of Michigan is out of business.

DON CANHAM

Well, I don't think you dehumanize an athlete if you give him a grant aid or a scholarship. You know in our country most of the scholarships that young people coming out of high school receive are based on need. We had a classic case in Michigan, where the student was a super student coming out of high school, but the priorities governmental and otherwise are based on need. Now, in intercollegiate athletics it's one of the areas, one of the few areas that I know where you base your aid on talents. You know these two countries were built on talents, and I see nothing wrong with rewarding talents. We have a number of regulations, university-wide and in the national collegiate athletics association of the Big 10, that protects the athletes. For instance, if an athlete comes to the University of Michigan on a grant aid, or a scholarship, or a ride, or whatever you want to call it, and breaks a leg and can't ever play again, he does not go off scholarship. We have six boys right now who haven't played a day of football, they will stay on scholarship until they graduate, and I guess what I am saying is, that there are some evils in intercollegiate athletics. There are evils in anything that you want to name, but I think the intercollegiate picture in the United States at least is better now, it protects the athlete more than any time that I can remember, and I have been around the sports scene for twenty years.

Question

What does Alan Eagleson think about the social desirability of commercialization of sports?

ALAN EAGLESON

This is something that the public determines, and I am convinced that as long as the NHL can continue to get away with its dilution of product and have fans come to attend. Then as players and representing them, we are going to demand as much as we can.

Question

Well, why don't you give them the message? Why don't you say listen our players are hung over, because they are flying to a hundred plus games a year and a hundred-thousand miles through the air, and they don't have enough time to practice any more and they don't have enough time to sleep any more. And, acclimatizing themselves to the time zone changes they are going through, and so they are playing lousy hockey. And, that is because the psychological results of the kind of expectations that capitalism is making upon professional sport.

ALAN EAGLESON

Let me give you the answer if I may, if I can, to that question. The National Hockey League televises the game on Sunday afternoons. The players association, and our meetings with the owners said that we didn't feel that there should be Sunday afternoon games hoisted upon teams when they played Saturday nights, and came out of different time zones. The simple answer was, well, alright we can do without that, and we are going to lose the television revenue which means that we have to cut down on the pension plan, and the players then made a choice. And, the players are in this position and we have seen the schedule go up from seventy games to seventy-eight games, in the same length of time. We have cut a training camp down from four-and-a-half to five weeks to three weeks. The players think the conditions aren't bad for the payment they are receiving. Until they revolt the owners are going to do the thing their way, and the players aren't interested in revolting at this stage, based on the salaries they are receiving.

Question

You said a minute ago that you think the salaries are too high right now.

ALAN EAGLESON

No. No. I said they may not be justified.

Question

In appreciation of Mr. Eagleson's efforts towards the players of all sports I think that we should applaud him, but I would like to ask one thing. On the other hand, haven't we gone too far over to the other side? I will take the example of the local teams in Detroit, and say the Lions for one thing. This year the Lions lost two games to New Orleans and Baltimore teams. They shouldn't have lost two. The coach tore the team apart, the owner tore the team apart. The team comes out the next week and gets a 34-0 victory. What does that accomplish? It seems today that the players have got so rich on their contracts that they perform when they feel like it. They exert as much effort as they feel, and you know if it isn't enough in that and if there is too much criticism, they can always jump to another league i.e., the WHA . . .

AL ACKERMAN

Is your question, are the players being very selfish, have the players got too pampered these days?

ALAN EAGLESON

I don't think so. It is a tough way to earn a dollar. Granted the dollars are high, these fellows aren't starving, but they have a talent that they have to exploit, it is a short term and when Louis Fontanto broke his back, he was well paid for five years. Suddenly he is a farmer with nothing to do. As far as motivation it doesn't relate not only to hockey, or to sports, it relates to business. Some people are not motivated in their work by anything. There are some hockey players like Orr and Espasito who I am sure would play for nothing. I wouldn't let Orr, but I am sure there are people that you know you say go to work at nine o'clock and leave at five will do it. Then there are others who if they don't think you are watching them all the time will get there at ten and leave at four. I might even be in the latter group myself. But, I think motivation is not only derived from money.

Question

Do you see women's participation in sport as an escape from the present commercialized ideal of femininity?

ABIGAIL HOFFMAN

I am not too sure if I am interpreting the question correctly, but I think what may be one of the things that the question is trying to get at is whether women are trying to establish for themselves some other kinds of sport activity other than a mere replica or duplication of the existing kind of sport opportunities that exist for men, which are sort of the models on which we have to go on.

I see two different trends certainly as far as many of the women in professional sports are concerned. I don't think that they are getting away as well as they might from the kinds of commercial ideas of traditional femininity. And, it always bothers me a great deal. This happens in Canada often, and in the States as well where many world championship figure skaters will turn professional and then must compete in the Ice Capades or another one of these skating festivals. Travelling circus routines, and the kind of skating that many women have to do in those kinds of ice shows is obnoxious. It is sort of cutsey-pie-beauty-queen kind of thing. And, often these women have been fantastic world champions and outstanding in their ability as skaters. When they get in the ice shows they really get very little opportunity to show the kind of ability that they really have. I do think, however, that there are other women at other levels of competition that are trying very hard to get away from the kind of standard concepts of what we have about what women should do and how women should behave. I think that in general just the increase in the number of women getting into sports indicates some sort of direction away from passive, non-aggressive activity.

"BOLAND MEMORIAL LECTURE"

Jesse Owens
Track Star and Author

J. Francis Leddy (Chairman)
President and Vice-Chancellor
University of Windsor

Jesse Owens
Olympic Track Star and Author

You know Dr. Murray when I got your letter some time ago, I had heard about Dr. Boland, I had heard about what he had done. Then when I found out that I was invited to come, I studied a little bit more about him. I began to understand what I was to do, and I began to think in terms of what it meant to be able to come, and I am sorry that I wasn't here today to hear many of the members of your panels that discussed the various aspects of athletics.

Athletics has become a way of life in the world. There are different depths to which different countries think in terms of the athletic world. In Canada, as in America, one sport which we have in common is football. It has become a way of life with all of us here. There is a Canadian and American version. It matters not about the version, but what does matter is when the contact comes and the thrill of touchdowns and the thrill of home runs. All of this adds to the impetus of what this game is all about.

In 1936, Dr. Leddy was eluding to this . . . we had a lot of fun in Germany. Thank God we weren't as politically orientated as the youngsters are today. We didn't have television. We didn't have the modern newspapers, or the magazines, that you have today, but we still have history, and Doctor, I just don't want anybody in here to forget any parts of their history, and certainly that part about Hitler, because if you will forget Hitler you will forget me and I am just too old for people to start forgetting.

I was talking to some people today, young people, and they wanted to know a little about 1936 in Germany. They had read in their history books about it, and they asked me about Hitler and they wanted to know if I knew him. I saw Hitler every day, and they wanted to know what did he look like? And, I said, "He looks just like any other man, he had a little moustache, and he did put his pants on one leg at a time just like we do here I think fellows." And, they wanted to know if I shook hands with him, and well, no, frankly I didn't shake hands with Hitler. In the first place, I didn't go over there to shake hands with him, Mr. Mayor. We went to run and run we did, and we had a marvellous time, and I am so sorry that he didn't. And, I am here in Windsor tonight having a marvellous time. I would like to say that I am very happy indeed to be in a country where people really believe in God. As you all know, Hitler did not believe in God. And, at the height of World War II, when the war was going rather badly for the German people, he called upon the people in whom he believed, and they were the astrologers. He asked the astrologers, "Am I going to lose the war?" and they said, "Yes, you are going to lose it." And, he wanted to know upon which day he was going to die. So they told him that he would die on a Jewish holiday. Then he wanted to know on which Jewish holiday he was going to die. They promptly told him, "Any day that you die will be a Jewish holiday."

Well, we woke up one lady out there.

Tonight I would like to talk about what makes the things Dr. Boland believed in work. I would like to talk to you about the young people, which is the greatest commodity any country in the world has today. I would like to talk to you about winning. What does it take to make a winner? And, what are we going to learn out of winning? I believe that your seminar today brought forth to you a number of different kinds of answers to what you are thinking about, and I am not here to contradict any of the conclusions, but to add something that I believe in, something that I have grown up with as the thing that makes the winner.

I can go back to my own junior high school days, and I can remember when I started my athletic career at age thirteen. I was in a junior high school, and we had a man that we revered, a man that we thought was the messiah. He could open up the waters, and we could walk on ground through the sea, simply because we believed in this man. I remember this man coming to our school and speaking to us on the 1924/1928 Olympic Games. He was telling us what a thrill it was and this is the beginning of my knowing about one of the greatest Olympians of all times in Canada, Percy Williams. Percy Williams was the 1928 Olympic champion in the 100 meters, and this man had competed against him. But, the man that spoke to us was known as the "world's fastest human being," and when he had finished, the youngsters lined up and they received an autograph. I was at the end of the line, and the coach invited me into his office. I sat in a chair and watched this man as he sat on the edge of the desk with one leg dangling down and he and the coach were conversing. When the man left, the coach said to me, "Well, what do you think?" I said, "Coach I would like to be me, and certainly I would like to be known as the world's fastest human being."

That was the beginning of the bit of philosophy and a better way of life that began for me on that day. Because, he sat there and he told me the ingredients to become a winner. The coach talked to me about determination, about how determined you must be reaching the dream that you have, and then he began to tell me about dedication. Being dedicated to a particular sport, and to the school I attended. Dedicated to the men and women of that institution of learning and the classroom, as well as the sidewalks that we ran upon. Being dedicated was vital. Then he began to talk to me about discipline, how well-disciplined was I going to be. Self-discipline was the ingredient that was going to make the worthwhile individual. I remembered those words, and I remember going through the things and listening to him as he talked to me about the proper methods of running.

It was the year 1936 . . . August 2nd, of that year thirty-seven years later as I think about it today. Thirty-seven years ago I stood at that starting line and I looked down that field at that hundred meters which is one-hundred-and-nine yards and two feet away, and then I remembered his words, and I thought about his counsel. I thought about his coaching, I thought about the family from which I had come. The city in which I had lived. Then I looked down at the uniform which I wore, and thinking in terms of the number of years that it took me to get there. Believing in this bit of philosophy that he had, knowing that all of it was going to go within ten seconds. It was a belief, and this was a belief that Dr. Boland had, that this banquet tonight and those of the years gone by, would leave an indelible impression upon the men and women that came and believed in a bit of philosophy in which he had. Evidently it left a great impression, because you are here in greater numbers today than ever before in the last fifteen years. So, therefore, it is beginning to have an understanding and a meaning, and what it is going to do. I think in terms of other people, and I think in terms of young people and what they have believed in order to make a reality or a dream come true.

I can remember being Director of a *Boys Club in Chicago,* and I can remember those youngsters that came from the ghetto of that city. Youngsters that lived in two and two-and-a-half, and at the most three-and-a-half rooms. Where there often times were seven, eight, nine, and ten and many times eleven people in a family living in no more than three-and-a-half rooms. I can remember those youngsters belonging to this club, not a pretentious one, but one that was much better than the home from which they had come. I can remember their interests, and I can remember their dedication, and their discipline within this club, where they wanted to make it the best club in the city of Chicago. Even though they did not have all of the facilities they had a heart, they had a soul, and they believed. I remember one year, it was 1950 when our government asked us to go to the European theatre of war (the operations of the European theatre of war), to study the rehabilitation of the young peoples of the European theatre of war. I remember staying there for two-and-a-half weeks and coming back and going to the State Department, and making my report to them and then hurrying to my home in Chicago to meet with my twenty-five young leaders of that club. I called them together at four o'clock in the afternoon, they were the ages of seven to seventeen. We had a little boy who was nine years old that was the spiritual leader of this club. As I talked to the State Department, and I related to them about the young men that were seventeen, eighteen, and nineteen years old who were assuming the full responsibility of manhood, because their fathers had gone away and would never return for the protection of the homes in which they lived.

They were here trying to protect their mothers and sisters and trying to remove the grim reminder of war by taking paint and cement and covering up the battle-scarred doors and the walls in the homes in which they lived. When I had finished my report to these twenty-five young leaders, this little boy whose legs were encased in braces because of a severe case of polio, gathered his crutches under his arm and struggled out of that chair and he stood upright, and he laid his crutches against my desk and he looked at me and he said, "Mr. Owens," he said, "many years ago in the halls and walls of this building there came some great men." The boy referred to men who were dedicated to a cause, men such as: Lionel Hampton, one of our great musicians of the time; Joe Louis, perhaps the greatest fighter of the time; Duke Ellington used to come and visit that club; and other great names that were in the walls and halls of this boys' club. The boy continued, "We have some happy memories, we believe in what we are doing. You have talked to us of how these other men became champions and on the walls of this building it tells us how to become winners." And, then he talked about dedication. He talked about discipline, and he talked about desire to be a winner. He said, "We don't have any money, we don't have anything financially that we can send to the young peoples of the European Theatre of War," he continued, "but, spiritually we can." And with that in mind, he took his little arms and he stretched them out, and then he raised his face skyward and he began to pray, and twenty-four boys dropped on one knee, and when the prayer was over, the twenty-four boys silently filed out of that room. And, he said to me, "We are dedicated to our club, but we need another ingredient to make it all possible. We need a little house of prayer." I said, "Why don't you go to the church next door?" He said, "I can't, because I don't have the proper clothing to wear. The others do not have it either." I said, "We have clothing in the basement that was given to us by churches and other organizations, and it is clean." He said, "I know that, but my Mother won't allow me to accept charity." There were six others in his family, there was no father. The mother made forty-two dollars and fifty cents a week. Of the forty-two dollars and fifty cents a week that she made, twenty-two dollars and fifty cents went weekly for the two-and-a-half rooms in which they lived. I said, "I can't fight you on that issue. But what made you say that we needed a little house of prayer? Who told you?" He said, "No one told me. I thought about it. I wanted it. I asked my Lord." "And," I asked, "what did you say to your Lord?" and he looked at me, with the palms of his hands on my desk, and he said:

Dear Lord, I come to you in prayer, and I have found hope and comfort there.

You gave me wisdom, courage, and power, that I so needed in that hour.

And, before I ask you knew my need, and the answer came with the fullest speed.

So graciously would love you feed, my soul of the necessary bread.

And, again dear Lord I come to pray, for guidance of help along the way,

Teach me things you have me know, and show me the way your child should go.

And, mold me, Oh God! so I may be prepared to serve more fittingly,

In the name of your dear Son, I asked your will be done.

We opened up that house of prayer, but you couldn't come, we opened it up on a Sunday morning. That Sunday morning we had three people, and I was one of the three. The following Sunday, we had a few more, and it wasn't many Sundays thereafter that we outgrew the room in the basement of this club, and we moved up into the reception room, and there we met for several months, and outgrew that and moved into the gymnasium and after eighteen months outgrew that. I asked a fraternal organization for the use of their auditorium on a Sunday morning, and that is where they are meeting today. But, you couldn't come unless you earned the right to come, and to earn the right to come you had to be a citizen of that community. You had to go to school every day, you had to know something about law and order, you had to know something about safety. Working with the fire and the police department and one of the pre-requisites was to stand before the supermarkets every Friday and Saturday and assist the women with their huge packages of groceries either to the home from which they had come or the automobile that brought them there. Your pay on that day was, "I want to thank you to be able to serve you, and may God bless."

When they met on a Sunday morning no one was allowed to put more than a nickel in the collection, and because of their work in that community and the love of their community and the determination to make it the best community in the city of Chicago. Juvenile delinquency dropped almost to nil. Women that lived out· side the area were now coming in to do their shopping, and the businessman's profits were growing and every Sunday morning they would send additional funds to this little house of prayer. Every Monday morning it was my good fortune to be able to walk with this little lad with his crutches and five members of his congregation. He didn't want to ride, he wanted to walk. They deposited every dime that they had taken in that Sunday, but the greatest joy was to go back the first of every month, and there they would sit down with the executive vice-president of the bank and would draw out every dime that they had placed the previous Sundays. Then they would go to *Care* and buy as many *Care* packages as their dollars would allow them to buy, to send to youngsters of other lands who they felt were less fortunate than they. That was their goal. That was their way of winning, that was their belief and their God to win. And, to give of themselves and the discipline that went along with it. I used to talk to them about what it meant to be a champion.

Yes, it is great that we should all strive to win. This is the ultimate but in winning there are other things, and Dr. Boland is looking from above and looking at you today and saying perhaps this is the thing. Championships, ladies and gentlemen, consist of very beautiful trophies that we might win. That's the number one prize. We will take that prize and put it in a place of honour in our institutions of learning. Oftentimes championships are made of very beautiful banners that we might win, which is a piece of cloth and materials, and we will take it and we will hang it upon the wall in a place of honour. Six months from today, that trophy simply because it is a piece of metal has become so corroded that you cannot read the year in which it was won. The banner that hangs upon the wall, symbolic of that championship is going to gather so much dust that you cannot read the year upon which it was won.

Well, what is important on the road to the championship is that we fight. As long as the child is going to learn in the classroom and he is going to learn upon the field of competition a code of ethics by which to live, that is what is important. He is going to learn how to spell the word respect, respect for the rights and properties of his fellow man. He learns to play the game of life as well as the game of athletics according to the rules of our society in which we live. If that child can take from the classroom and from the floor of the field of competition and put it into practice in the community in which he lives, then to me that child has won the greatest championship that any person can ever win! These are the things that shall never become tarnished. These are the things that shall never gather dust, and these are the things that will live with that child as long as he lives on the face of God's earth.

This to me is the basis of what it means to compete, of what it means to be a winner, and of what it means to know something about his fellow man. As long as he is playing the game, as a team sport or an individual sport he is able to walk and talk to his fellow man. They might be miles apart in their thinking, but as long as they walk and they talk, they broaden understanding. They understand each other's problems, and then we build that thing we call the brotherhood of man. This is what Dr. Boland, in my opinion, as I know him, believed in: love of humanity, love of fellow citizen, belief in what competition can bring about. I think this Seminar has a great meaning for all whom are concerned, believing.

Finally, I know a man that lives this kind of life. I knew him for many years. I used to watch him run three miles before he ran the official mile, and I wanted to try. But, I noticed on his body many scars, and I wanted to know about those scars, and they began to tell me about him. When he was eleven years old he was burnt so badly that the doctors said that if he lived that he would never walk again, but this boy wanted to walk, and he wanted to live. He was determined that he was going to walk, he was disciplined to believe in it. Dedicated enough to the sport that he wanted to run, and when he got out of the hospital after fourteen months of skin grafts he started to walk and as he walked his body would bleed, and his mother would re-wrap the body again and he would walk again, and bleed again and she continued to wrap his blood until he bled no longer, and then he ran. He started to run, and the pressures would break the skin, and the body would bleed, and he would continue to run until he would bleed no longer. In 1936 he was a teammate of mine, he did not win the coveted prize. He got a second place in the fifteen hundred meters, but he was proud of that silver medal. He came back to America, and then he started to teach, he started to think about his dream, and he turned out great athletes, some were representatives in the 1948 Games, some in 1952. He just hadn't fulfilled his dream of helping humanity. He started to travel this country, he started to travel America, he found some land, and some friends of his helped him buy land. On the land they built a church, they built the house, they built the school, and they built cottages, and they stocked it with animals. A child came down the highway from a broken home, a child that did not have the feeling of belonging or the feeling of being needed, or a child that did not have love. He took that child in for fourteen to fifteen months. He gave that child an animal. He taught that child love, he taught him how to be able to discipline himself. He taught him about determination, and dedication. At the end of that fifteen or sixteen months that child would leave, becoming a citizen of this land, knowing where he wanted to go. That man is winning gold medals day after day. He stands before podiums of this kind day after day, and the money derived from his speeches goes back to the ranch to help another five or six hundred people year in and year out. Gold medals every day. Simply because he wanted to be a winner, and that was his method of becoming a greater winner for humanity.

So you see, there are many ways, many ways that one can become a winner, and I am no different than you. Yes, I wanted to become a winner. Yes, it was my August 2nd, and I certainly hope that this will become your August 2nd.

Thirty-seven years ago, as I said before as I stood at that starting line and looking down that hundred and nine yards and two feet away flanked with seven other men, and every man in there was a potential winner. Every man wanted to become a winner, and the person that won it, of course, was given the title of the world's fastest human being. Realizing that it was all going to go within a short time, nine years it took me to get there, and I can recall that race because I can remember the starter. I remember the starter as we sat there on that bench. I looked around that stadium and I noticed the green grass and a red track with the white lines. As my eyes went into the stands I noticed a hundred and some odd thousand people sitting and standing within that great arena. My eyes went upward again, I noticed a flag of every nation that was represented there at the Olympic Games underneath that blue German sky. My attention was diverted from that beautiful picture because the whistle had been blown, and we were to assemble around the starter to receive our final instructions for this most historic event. After our instructions had been given, the starter stepped back about ten paces and he hollered loudly in German, "Auf die Plätze," every man went to his mark, adjusting his hands and feet. The starter suddenly said in a soft voice, "fertig," and every man came to a set position, every muscle in his body was strained, and the gun went off. The boys ran neck and neck for fifty yards. Ralph Metcalfe of Marquette University leading the field to the fifty yard mark, and from the seventy to the ninety Ralf and I ran neck and neck, and for some unknown reason, I beat Ralf Metcalfe from Marquette University in this historic event.

The greatest honour came as we stood up there on that pedestal of victory, and after we had knelt and received the wreath of victory from the German maidens, and standing there facing the stands from a far away distance you could hear the strains of the *Star Spangled Banner*. As the people in the stands stood, the Germans gave the Nazi salute, the Americans gave the American salute, and as we three on the pedestal of victory we angled our faces. Yes, I noticed the Stars and Stripes were rising higher and higher. The higher the Stars and Stripes rose, yes the louder the strains of the *Star Spangled Banner* were heard. On that day I stood there and I thought about nine years earlier listening to what the coach had said about a dream, and from that day I could say today I am an Olympic Champion. It was my August 2nd, thirty-seven years ago.

So this is your day, your Seminar Dr. Murray, something that Dr. Boland thought about many years ago, and let's make it his August 2nd in years to come. Simply because we believe in order to be winners there comes a point of dedication, discipline, and determination of where we want to go.

I am thankful for the opportunity of breaking bread with you on this night, and with your permission may I say to the assembled as they leave here and go back to the homes from which they come, my prayer is that "May God ride with you and may he walk with you, and may he continue to give you the guidance and understanding for the privilege that we have to live upon this earth."

As He looks from above to us, his children below, we at this Seminar can truly look back and say, "Yes, O God, from the knowledge of this day we will give you a better world, and a better place for mankind to live."

"THE NORTH AMERICAN SYNDROME: SPORT FOR ADULTS—ATHLETICS FOR CHILDREN"

John Loy
Sociologist
University of Massachusetts

Cecil Eaves
Development Coordinator
Amateur Sports CAHA

Frank Wansbrough (Chairman)
Mayor of Windsor

John Loy
Sociologist
University of Massachusetts

At the outset of the program today I should like to express my admiration for the cunningness of the conference organizers. The sagacious selection of the theme for the seminar and the topic for this session clearly reveals their Machiavellian nature. They have employed several strategies to insure that every speaker will find himself in a quandary. One effective ploy is their use of dichotomies like "sport versus athletics" and "adults versus children" which pose the difficult problem of dealing or not dealing with "the excluded middle."

A second successful ploy is their use of provocative terms such as "dilemma" and "syndrome" which force discussants to assume unnatural advocative positions. I am particularly hooked on the horns of the "North American Dilemma" which serves as the focal point for the conference. The term dilemma denotes an argument necessitating a choice between equally disagreeable alternatives, and I am equally disinclined to accept or reject the underlying assumption of the seminar theme that athletics has preempted sport as the primary form of agonetic behavior.

I face a similar problem with the "North American Syndrome." The term syndrome denotes a combination of symptoms which characterize a specific disease, and I am not certain that the supposition "sport for adults, athletics for children" suggests a sick state of affairs. More specifically, I am equally unwilling to accept or reject the underlying assumption that adult involvement in agonetic activities is characterized by a *satisfaction* orientation, i.e., "sport for sport's sake," whereas the involvement of children in competitive physical activity is characterized by a *success* orientation, i.e., "winning for winning sake."

In short, I submit that in order to discuss adequately the assumptions associated with the thesis "sport for adults, athletics for children" we must empirically examine four interrelated issues. Expressed in interrogative form, these issues are:

First, "to *what* degree are individuals actively engaged in agonetic activities?" Is there in fact a high percentage of North Americans who are highly involved in sport and athletics other than vicariously?

Second, "*who* is actively engaged in agonetic activities?" That is, what social categories of persons are most involved in competitive physical activity? Is game involvement greatly influenced by such social identities as age, sex, and social status?

Third, "*how* are individuals actively engaged in agonetic activities?" That is, what types of agonetic activities do people prefer to participate in, and at what competitive level are they so engaged? Are children more highly involved in athletics than adults?

Fourth, "*why* are individuals actively engaged in agonetic activities?" That is, what types of psychological dispositions are directly associated with participation in sport and athletics? Do adults place greater emphasis on personal satisfaction in sport competition, and children give greater stress to the importance of social success in athletic competition?

I shall discuss the four issues set forth in terms of three broad categories of participants; namely, adults, young adults and youth. The evidence I bring to bear will of necessity be both scanty and selective. However, I hope that my remarks will raise a number of issues for the discussion which is to follow.

Adult Participation in Cross-National Perspective

The primacy of sport and athletics in the mass media of North America has led many individuals, including most physical educators, to believe that a substantial proportion of adults actively participate in sport, and that a majority of adults often attend athletic events. Several surveys of some scope suggest that these assumptions should be seriously questioned.

I first became aware of the low rates of active participation among adults when I assisted Gerald Kenyon (1966) in sampling the adult population of the State of Wisconsin in order to ascertain the significance of physical activity in the lifestyles of American adults. Kenyon examined the degree of primary and secondary participation in light, moderate and vigorous physical activity for fall, winter and summer seasons. He discovered that only a minority of Wisconsin adults (i.e., non-institutionalized men and women over the age of 21) actively engaged in physical activity. For example, he found that during the summer months less than 7 percent of the men and only 5 percent of the women engaged in "vigorous" physical activities at least once per week. Moreover, in the summer only 29 percent of the men and 21 percent of the women attended sporting events in person once a month or more often.

Kenyon's findings at the state level have been corroborated at the national level. Robinson has reported results of time-budget data consisting of ". . . a census of *all* daily adult activities on a "typical" day in ten European countries, Peru and the United States" (1970, p. 156). His findings concerning the amount of daily free time and minutes spent on sport involvement are summarized in Table 1. It is evident from the table that although American adults have some daily five hours of free time, less than six minutes of this free time are devoted to sport involvement when men and

Table 1

DAILY FREE TIME* AND ADULT PARTICIPATION IN
ACTIVE SPORTS IN 12 COUNTRIES

Country	Total Sample Total Free Time	Total Free Time on Sports	Time Spent		Participation Rates	
	Time	*Sports*	*Men*	*Women*	*Men*	*Women*
Belgium	297	2.0	3.5	.5	3.8%	.8%
Bulgaria	231	2.1	2.8	.9	8.2	2.8
Czechoslovakia	239	2.2	3.5	1.1	5.2	1.9
East Germany	233	1.3	2.4	.6	3.4	1.9
France	245	1.4	2.4	.4	4.0	1.2
Hungary	200	1.5	2.7	.4	3.6	1.0
Peru	309	1.6	2.5	.9	4.1	1.8
Poland	262	1.0	1.8	.3	5.5	2.1
Russia	249	4.7	6.9	3.0	29.7	13.0
U.S. (Jackson)	310	5.0	7.1	3.2	5.1	4.4
U.S. (National)	301	5.5	8.2	3.3	7.8	4.0
West Germany (Osnabrück)	300	4.0	4.3	3.8	5.5	5.0
West Germany (National)	264	5.4	7.7	3.6	5.8	3.5
Yugoslavia (Maribor)	222	1.8	4.0	.1	4.6	.7
Yugoslavia (Kragujevac)	311	.2	.3	.0	.9	.3

* Time is expressed in minutes per day.
SOURCE: Robinson, 1970, p. 162.

women are considered together. An analysis of the data by sex shows that men are twice as active in sports as women. However, actual participation rates are nearly identical to the low rates found by Kenyon. Robinson further reports that: (1) bowling is the most popular active (?) sport for American adults; (2) only two percent of Americans take part in exercises and only one percent engage in strenuous sports on an average day; and, (3) well over 50 percent of the sample stated that they had not participated in any active sport the previous year and another tenth had done so less than five times (1970, pp. 167-168). Although Robinson does not report why people are motivated to participate in physical activity, he does give figures for the degree of satisfaction men and women derive from engagement in sports and games. Table 2 shows that women do not receive a great deal of satisfaction from sport involvement, and both men and women appear to obtain more satisfaction from watching sport events than by playing active sports.

As a third illustration of the limited active sport involvement of American adults, I refer to the National Recreation Survey conducted by the Outdoor Recreation Resources Review Commission (Ferriss, 1962). The ORRRC Study determined the degree of sport participation of persons 12 years and over in the United States during June-August 1960. Table 3 shows the percentage of persons participating in various outdoor pursuits during the summer of 1960. The table reveals that the related activities of swimming, boating and fishing are the most popular leisure activities. However, it is evident that many active sports have few participants. Moreover, one should view with caution the finding that nearly a third of the population was involved in playing outdoor sports. A detailed examination of this finding is made in Table 4 where the figures recorded in Table 3 are broken down by age, sex and relative days of participation. Table 4 clearly shows that participation in outdoor games and sports is largely confined to young males, and also reveals a limited number of days of actual participation.

Table 2

SPORT PARTICIPATION AND PERSONAL SATISFACTION —
FOR NATIONAL SAMPLE OF AMERICAN ADULTS

Degree of Satisfaction	Great	Much	Some	Little	None
Men (%)	43	28	16	6	7
Women (%)	14	16	28	19	23

CORRELATIONS BETWEEN DEGREE OF SATISFACTION
AND SPECIFIC AGONETIC ACTIVITIES

Activity	Men	Women
Watch Sport Events	.30	.29
Play Active Sports	.23	.27
Hunting, Fishing, etc.	.09	.15
Play Cards, etc.	.12	.15

SOURCE: Robinson, 1970, pp. 170-171.

Table 3

SPORT PARTICIPATION OF PERSONS 12 YEARS AND OVER
IN THE UNITED STATES DURING JUNE-AUGUST 1960

Activity		Region (%)			
	US	NE	NC	S	W
1. Playing Outdoor Sports	30	34	35	21	28
2. Camping	8	5	7	8	17
3. Hunting	3	2	2	5	3
4. Fishing	29	21	33	33	30
5. Canoeing	2	3	3	2	1
6. Sailing	2	2	2	1	2
7. Other Boating	22	21	27	19	23
8. Swimming	45	53	42	40	48
9. Water Skiing	6	4	6	6	9
10. Mountain Climbing	1	2	1	1	1
11. Hiking	6	7	5	4	9
12. Horseback Riding	6	4	5	5	11
13. Bicycling	9	9	10	7	10
14. Nature Walks	14	15	15	12	16
15. Attending Outdoor Sports Events	24	22	28	21	26

SOURCE: National Recreation Survey, ORRRC Study Report 19, 1962, p. 120.

Table 4

PERCENT OF PERSONS 12 YEARS AND OVER PARTICIPATING
IN OUTDOOR GAMES AND SPORT DURING JUNE-AUGUST 1960

Category		Region			
	US	NE	NC	S	W
1. All Categories	30	34	35	21	28
2. Males (age in years)	34	42	37	25	33
a. 12-17	70	70	70	69	70
b. 18-24	50	72	54	25	60
c. 25-44	37	48	42	24	29
d. 45-64	18	22	20	11	19
e. 65 and over	2	2	3	1	5
3. Females (age in years)	25	27	32	17	24

a. 12-17	64	70	64	59	64
b. 18-24	44	47	62	31	32
c. 25-44	25	28	34	12	28
d. 45-64	9	11	13	5	6
e. 65 and over	2	4	1	1	.5
4. Race					
a. White	30	34	34	21	27
b. Non-white	29	30	46	21	42
Days per Person	3.6	3.9	4.2	2.9	3.4
Days per Participant	12.3	11.6	12.0	13.9	12.0

SOURCE: National Recreation Survey, *ORRRC Study Report 19,* 1962, p. 134.

Having looked at the American picture, let me turn to the Canadian scene. Recent analysis of national data on leisure-time physical and sports activities in Canada by James Curtis and Brian Milton of the University of Waterloo indicate that Canadian society is as nearly "sedentary" as American society (cf. Curtis and Milton, 1973; and, Milton, 1973). Table 5 shows the percent of adult Canadians participating in active sports during 1972. Like the United States participation is highest among young adults, and more particularly young males. Table 6 is more revealing in that it shows the percent of Canadian adults engaged in specific sports in season. As can be seen from the table, active involvement is largely restricted to walking, swimming, fishing and hunting.

In summary, a strong case can be made that only a minority of North American adults actively participate in sport. Interestingly, several of the sports adults are most involved in represent work and survival activities that have been transformed into play forms; as for example, fishing, hunting, boating and swimming (see Stone, 1955 for a discussion of these transformations).

The type of agonetic activities favored by adults in the studies cited support the thesis underlying this session; namely, "sport for adults, athletics for children." Unfortunately, the principal investigators of the studies discussed did not attempt to ascertain the motivations of the minority of adults directly participating in physical activity. Thus we have no indication as to whether adults primarily participate for reasons of play and satisfaction, or for the reasons of competition and success via winning outcomes. However, a recent national survey of patterns of participation in outdoor and physical recreation among people living in the urban areas of England and Wales (Sillitoe, 1969) shows that the primary attractions and incentives for sport involvement among adults are expressive rather than instrumental in nature. For example, for all males combined (15 years of age to 46 and over) the attractions of outdoor or physical recreation in order of their importance were found to be:

Table 5

PERCENT OF ADULT CANADIANS PARTICIPATING
IN ACTIVE SPORTS DURING 1972 (N=53, 294)

Sport	Playing Sports in Winter[a]		Playing Sports in Season[b]	
Category	Low	High	Low	High
1. Total Sample	82.0	7.6	36.7	37.1
2. Male	78.0	10.3	31.4	43.9
3. Female	85.7	5.1	41.2	31.1
4. 20-34 years	74.8	10.5	27.8	48.7
5. 35-54 years	88.3	5.1	42.9	28.2
6. 55 and older	96.3	1.9	56.6	11.9

[a]High activity represents 4 or more hours per week, and low activity represents less than 1 hour per week.

[b]High activity represents 2 or more sports, low activity represents no sports.
SOURCE: Milton, 1973, Table 1.

Table 6

PERCENT OF ADULT CANADIANS INVOLVED IN SPECIFIC
SPORTS IN SEASON DURING 1972 (N=53, 294)

Sport	Category Total	Male	Female	20-34 yrs.	35-54 yrs.	55 yrs.+
1. Walking	37.7	34.1	41.0	38.4	36.4	37.6
2. Swimming	22.5	24.0	21.0	31.8	14.3	3.4
3. Fishing/Hunting	20.3	31.8	9.4	23.9	18.8	8.8
4. Snowmobiling	10.2	12.8	7.8	14.8	6.0	1.3
5. Bowling	9.7	9.9	9.5	12.9	7.0	3.3
6. Skating	9.5	10.9	8.1	15.2	3.1	1.0
7. Bicycling	6.9	6.4	7.3	9.7	4.1	1.6
8. Golf	6.9	10.3	3.6	8.1	6.7	2.2
9. Curling	4.8	6.0	3.7	5.8	4.5	1.5
10. Rec. Hockey	4.8	8.3	1.6	7.4	2.0	1.2
11. Snow Skiing	4.5	5.1	3.8	6.8	2.0	0.8
12. Jogging	4.2	5.3	3.1	5.8	2.7	1.2
13. Water Skiing	3.8	5.0	2.6	5.8	1.5	0.7
14. Tennis	3.0	3.4	2.6	4.6	1.2	0.6
15. Other Sports	6.4	8.4	4.5	9.0	3.7	1.9

SOURCE: Milton, 1973, Table 5.

(1) keeping fit, (2) the open air, (3) the chance to mix with people, (4) the pleasure of competition, and (5) takes your mind off things.

For all females combined the order of incentives was: (1) the chance to mix with other people, (2) the open air, (3) keeping fit, (4) takes your mind off things, and (5) the pleasure of competition (Sillitoe, 1969, p. 172). Like their North American counterparts, only a minority of British adults are actively engaged in physical activity and those who are involved favor such activities as swimming, dancing, bowling and fishing (Sillitoe, 1969, p. 236 and p. 238).

Having briefly examined patterns of adult participation, let me turn to that group of young North American adults represented by college and university students.

Young Adult Participation in Cross-National Perspective

Intercollegiate athletics are a major commercial enterprise in the United States involving thousands of students in active competition. But, as can be readily inferred from Tables 7, 8 and 9 involvement in intercollegiate athletics is confined to a small percentage of male undergraduates competing in a limited number of sports. For example, in 1966-67 over 154,000 male students engaged in intercollegiate athletics compared to less than 16,000 women; and these 170,000 students in combination comprised only 4 percent of the total undergraduate population of over 4,000,000 students. In sum, only a minority of college and university students are engaged in highly competitive sports that we might denote as athletics.

Like their adult counterparts, most college students participating in active sports might be best termed "daily duffers." These daily duffers are to be found in intramural competition and recreational clubs (see Table 9 for an estimate of this population). Recent work by Brian Petrie of the University of Western Ontario provides a great deal of insight concerning the motivations for participation in agonetic activities by members of that student population I have labelled daily duffers. In one study Petrie (1971a) surveyed a ran-

Table 7

INTERCOLLEGIATE ATHLETICS FOR MEN IN THE U.S. (1966-67)

Type of Sport	Number of Institutions		Number of Participants
1. Football	(6)	477	36,799
2. Track & Field	(4)	484	18,967

3.	Baseball	(3) 527	17,101
4.	Basketball	(1) 576	15,247
5.	Soccer	(10) 277	10,370
6.	Swimming	(8) 312	8,269
7.	Wrestling	(9) 332	7,889
8.	Tennis	(2) 515	7,155
9.	Cross Country	(7) 428	6,281
10.	Golf	(5) 466	6,160

SOURCE: NCAA, *Report No. 3*, 1968, p. 4.

Table 8

WOMEN'S INTERCOLLEGIATE AND EXTRAMURAL ATHLETICS
IN THE UNITED STATES (1966-67)

	Type of Sport	*Number of Institutions*	*Number of Participants*
1.	Basketball	217	4,253
2.	Field Hockey	137	3,126
3.	Volleyball	114	2,178
4.	Softball	60	1,366
5.	Tennis	137	1,361
6.	Swimming	68	1,184
7.	Gymnastics	47	579
8.	Golf	37	384
9.	Fencing	23	325
10.	Track & Field	28	309

SOURCE: NCAA, *Report No. 3*, 1968, p. 13.

Table 9

COMPARISON OF COLLEGE MEN'S AND WOMEN'S INVOLVEMENT
IN ACTIVE SPORTS IN THE U.S. (1966-67)

	Type of Participation	*Number of Men*	*Number of Women*
1.	Intercollegiate Athletics	154,179	15,727
2.	Intramural Competition	1,273,908	165,081
3.	Recreational Clubs	54,205	22,635
4.	Required Physical Education	527,302	409,860

SOURCE: NCAA, *Report No. 3*, 1968.

dom sample of 988 undergraduates of Michigan State University. In a second study he surveyed a random sample of 1,161 undergraduates at the University of Western Ontario. In both studies Petrie assessed the percentage of positive rankings given by respondents to ten primary reasons for participating in physical activity; in addition, he determined the degree to which students held a "play" or a "professional" orientation toward participation in competitive physical activities. The latter assessment was made using Webb's (1969) Professionalization Index which differentially weights responses to the question: "What do you think is most important in playing a game? (a) to play it as well as you are able, (b) to beat your opponent, (c) to play it fairly.

The results of Petrie's investigations are summarized in Tables 10, 11 and 12. Findings for American and Canadian samples are very similar. Although female students in both countries give higher positive rankings to "expressive motivations" while male students give higher positive rankings to "instrumental motivations", the overall orientation of these daily duffers is a "satisfaction" orientation rather than a "success" orientation. For example, even though a much greater percentage of American and Canadian males hold a professional or winning orientation toward sport involvement than female students, over three-fourths of the Canadian males and over four-fifths of the American males express a "play orientation" toward participation in competitive physical activity (see Table 12).

Unfortunately, Petrie's tenfold classification of motivations and Webb's professionalization index have not been used to compare comparable samples of American and Canadian intercollegiate athletes. Thus it is only assumption at this point that students competing in athletics stress attitudes reflecting an instrumental orientation of winning and success while students playing sports emphasize attitudes reflecting an expressive orientation of fun, social interaction and personal satisfaction. Moreover, at least one study leads one to seriously question this assumption.

Table 10

MOTIVATIONS FOR PARTICIPATION IN PHYSICAL ACTIVITY
AMONG AMERICAN UNIVERSITY STUDENTS[a] (N=625)

	Motivation	Positive N	Rankings %	Higher Group Rankings
1.	Fun and Enjoyment	602	96.32	*Female*
2.	Health	569	91.04	Male
3.	Competition in Skill	495	79.20	Male
4.	Social Interaction	433	69.28	*Female*
5.	Competition Against Environment	325	52.00	Male
6.	Aesthetic	309	49.44	*Female*

7. Risk	153	24.48	Male
8. Chance	79	12.64	Male
9. Skill with Weapon	75	12.00	Male
10. Competition in Combat	62	9.92	Male

aRandom sample of undergraduates at Michigan State University

SOURCE: Petrie, 1971a, pp. 93-94.

Table 11

MOTIVATIONS FOR PARTICIPATING IN PHYSICAL ACTIVITY AMONG CANADIAN UNIVERSITY STUDENTS[a] (N=826)

Motivation	Positive N	Rankings %	Higher Group Rankings
1. Fun and Excitement	783	97.38	*Female*
2. Health	768	95.64	*Female*
3. Competition in Skill	660	82.08	Male
4. Social Interaction	614	76.36	*Female*
5. Aesthetic	362	45.08	*Female*
6. Competition Against Environment	353	43.96	Male
7. Risk	184	22.88	Male
8. Competition in Combat	118	14.69	Male
9. Skill with Weapon	79	9.85	Male
10. Chance	66	8.20	Male

aRandom sample of undergraduates at the University of Western Ontario.

SOURCE: Petrie, 1971b, pp. 10-11.

Table 12

ATTITUDES TOWARD PLAY AMONG AMERICAN AND CANADIAN UNIVERSITY STUDENTS

Sex	American Students[a]		Total
	Play Orientation	*Professional Orientation*	
Male (303)	87.8	12.2	100
Female (314)	98.4	1.6	100

Sex	Canadian Students[b]		Total
	Play Orientation	*Professional Orientation*	
Male (502)	77.1	22.9	100
Female (306)	94.7	5.3	100

aPetrie, 1971a, p. 97.

bPetrie, 1971b, p. 12.

Richard Alderman (1970) administered Kenyon's Attitude Toward Physical Activity inventory to 136 Canadian athletes participating at the 1967 Pan-American Games in Winnipeg, Manitoba. Results of his study which are summarized in Table 13 show that similar attitudes are held toward physical activity by male and female athletes. Most surprisingly, the "aesthetic" attitude held first rank for men as well as women. And as noted by Alderman in conclusion: "a very low or weak response toward physical activity as an *ascetic* activity was predominant and indicated that, though long, strenuous, solitary training is probably necessary in most sports, there is not necessarily a strong positive corresponding attitude toward it" (1970, p. 9).

In sum, then, only a minority of young adults are involved in highly organized competitive athletics, and the majority of college and university students who engage in active sports do so for expressive reasons of fun and satisfaction rather than for instrumental reasons of achieving success through victory. As time marches on, let me quickly turn to a cursory review of the participation patterns of children and youth.

Participation of Youth in Cross-National Perspective

Although data on most aspects of competitive sports in childhood and early adolescence are limited, numerous statistics could be cited which support the contention that "athletics" is the primary form of agonetic activity among youth. At the high school level more money is spent on sport and athletics than any other phase of the program. And at the elementary school and junior high school level one finds a substantial number of varsity-type athletic programs. For example, a recent national survey conducted by the AAPHER Committee on Desirable Athletic Competition for Children of Elementary School Age (1968) shows that 83 percent of the schools organized on a K-8 basis support interschool competitive basketball programs.

Table 13

ATTITUDES TOWARD PHYSICAL ACTIVITY AMONG
CHAMPION CANADIAN ATHLETES[a] (N=136)

Male Athletes (n=81)

Attitude	Mean
1. Aesthetic	41.98
2. Catharsis	41.68

3.	Social	38.36
4.	Fitness	38.30
5.	Vertigo	36.84
6.	Ascetic	35.52

Female Athletes (n=55)

	Attitude	Mean
1.	Aesthetic	45.11
2.	Social	41.66
3.	Catharsis	40.87
4.	Fitness	40.42
5.	Ascetic	36.96
6.	Vertigo	32.64

[a]Participants from 10 sports at the 1967 Pan-American Games.

SOURCE: Alderman, 1970, p. 4.

Figures for athletic competition during childhood are most overwhelming when one examines competitive sport programs sponsored by community agencies outside the school. For example, in 1968 there were 1,865,000 eight-to-twelve year old boys participating in Little League Baseball, and 163,700 thirteen-to-fifteen year old boys playing Babe Ruth League baseball; not to mention the Stan Musial League, the Connie Mack League, and the Junior, Pony and Colt leagues sponsored by the Boys' Baseball organization. In 1969 there were some 600,000 boys aged 7-15 participating in Pop Warner Football leagues, and over 500,000 boys and girls 9 years and older engaged in age group swimming contests sponsored by the AAU. Age group competition is found in a variety of other sports, sponsored by such organizations as the U.S. Football Soccer Association, the U.S. Lawn Tennis Association, the U.S. Golf Association, the American Bowling Congress and the Women's International Bowling Congress. Perhaps the most competitive sport program for youth is the National Junior Olympic Program begun by the AAU in 1967. The intensity of competition is reflected in the fact that in 1967 a four year old girl won the six-and-under two mile swim in twenty-five minutes. I am not familiar with the Canadian scene but I am sure that members of the panel or audience could site similar statistics and examples for age group hockey competition.

In view of the theme of the session, "sport for adults, athletics for children," what needs to be determined is whether the many forms of "kid sports" are more for the children or mostly for the parents. Do many fathers without a claim to fame seek a name through the athletic prowess of their sons? If such be the case, then it is rather a false hope as few children go on to higher levels of competition. A recent report by the U.S. Department of Labor reveals that 400,000 out of some 2,000,000 Little League Baseball players go on to play high school ball, only about 25,000 go on to college ball, approximately 1,200 are in turn drafted by pro teams and perhaps 100 of these make it to the majors for at least a try (cf. *"Few and Far Between,"* 1973).

Again, as in the case of adults and college students I don't want to fix my attention on either the athlete or the nonparticipant, but rather wish to direct my attention to the average sports minded youth, or daily duffer if you will. I assume that other members of the panel will take up in earnest the problem of over-emphasis on athletics for children. I note in passing, however, that Dr. Lawrence Rarick deals with the matter at some length in the concluding chapter of a book he has recently edited for Academic Press entitled: *Physical Activity: Human Growth and Development* (1973).

A cross-national comparison of secondary school students involvement in physical activity shows major differences between boys and girls in terms of the most preferred sport for primary involvement, but reveals a high degree of similarity of preferred choices among students of the same sex. Tables 14 and 15 summarize selected data collected by Kenyon (1968) in a study of "values held for physical activity by selected urban secondary school students in Canada, Australia, England and the United States." Table 14 shows that both lower and upper division high school girls in America Canada rank social dance as their most preferred form of physical activity, while lower and upper division boys in the two countries cite football as their preferred active sport. Interestingly, similarities between American and Canadian students are also shown for Australian and English students, thus suggesting a Western youth subculture as regards sport styles. Table 15 indicates that American and Canadian youth also hold similar attitudes toward their favorite sports for primary involvement. Although physical activity as an ascetic experience receives the most positive rankings (a male bias), it is balanced by the second and third place rankings of physical activity as a social experience and as an experience of catharsis (a female bias).

As members of the seminar have by now surmised, I have attempted to find comparable studies of participation patterns and motivations for participation for various age groups of Americans

Table 14

CROSS-NATIONAL COMPARISON OF SECONDARY SCHOOL STUDENTS INVOLVEMENT IN PHYSICAL ACTIVITY: MOST PREFERRED SPORT FOR PRIMARY INVOLVEMENT (IN PERCENT OF THOSE RESPONDING)[a]

Sex and Level	Rank	United States		Canada		England		Australia	
Lower — Division Males	1	Amer. football	41	Can. football	24	Soccer	39	Aust. rugby	34
	2	basketball	15	ice hockey	16	swimming	19	swimming	15
	3	baseball	10	swimming	13	cricket	9	soccer	11
Upper — Division Males	1	Amer. football	39	Can. football	29	soccer	23	Aust. rugby	28
	2	basketball	19	ice hockey	16	rugby	13	swimming	13
	3	baseball	12	swimming	11	swimming	10	field hockey	11
Lower — Division Females	1	social dance	26	social dance	25	social dance	28	swimming	30
	2	swimming	19	swimming	20	swimming	18	social dance	18
	3	basketball	9	equestrian	9	tennis	14	basketball	16
Upper — Division Females	1	social dance	26	social dance	27	social dance	20	swimming	26
	2	basketball	16	swimming	19	tennis	20	basketball	19
	3	swimming	14	skiing	8	badminton	11	social dance	16

[a]SOURCE: Kenyon, 1968, pp. 82-83.

Table 15

CROSS-NATIONAL COMPARISON OF SECONDARY SCHOOL INVOLVEMENT IN PHYSICAL ACTIVITY: ATTITUDES HELD TOWARD FAVORITE SPORT FOR PRIMARY INVOLVEMENT[a] (In %)

Country	Ascetic	Catharsis	Social	Vertigo	Aesthetic	Health	Chance	Unclassified	n
U.S.A.	54	24	15	3	1	0	0	3	653
Canada	36	32	16	12	2	0	0	2	924
England	33	38	14	4	3	0	0	8	774
Australia	42	34	10	3	0	1	0	10	166
All	40	32	15	7	2	0	0	4	2,517

[a] SOURCE: Kenyon, 1968, p. 152.

and Canadians. Thanks to the helpful assistance of my Canadian colleagues Gerald Kenyon, Brian Milton (a Scottish transplant) and Brian Petrie (an Australian transplant) I have been relatively successful in my effort. A notable exception has been my failure to find comparable data for the ten and under age groupings. However, in closing my account of age group sport participation I would like to refer to three studies which illustrates the attitudes held toward play among American and Canadian preadolescents.

Webb (1969) investigated the professionalization of attitude toward play by surveying random samples of students enrolled in the public and parochial schools of Battle Creek, Michigan in 1967. At each grade level (3, 6, 8, 10 and 12) he asked students to rank in order of importance what they thought was personally most important in playing a game; to play it as well as you can, to beat your opponent, or to play the game fairly. Results of his study which are summarized at the top of Table 16 show the diminishing importance of the fairness factor and the increasing importance of the success factor (i.e., beating one's opponent) as age increases.

Results substantially similar to those reported by Webb were obtained by Maloney and Petrie (1972) in their study of the professionalization of attitude toward play among 567 Canadian schoolchildren in Grades 8, 9, 10 and 12. They found that:

(i) the males were more professionalized in their attitudes toward play than the females . . .; (ii) the professionalization of attitude toward play increased among the male students as they progressed through school; (iii) those respondents who had the greatest degree of involvement in athletic participation were more professionalized in their orientations toward physical activity; (iv) participation in intramural programs appeared to act as a damper upon the development of professionalized attitude toward play, regardless of the level of personal involvement in other sport forms (1972, p. 184).

Their findings concerning sex differences in the attitude held toward play are summarized at the bottom of Table 16.

Finally, I note that Maloney and Petrie's discovery that the professionalization of attitude toward play is directly related to degree of involvement in athletics is supported by a recent study of American preadolescent boys conducted by Mantel and Vander-Velden (1971). They compared 73 participants in organized sport

Table 16

PROFESSIONALIZATION OF ATTITUDE TOWARD PLAY AMONG
AMERICAN AND CANADIAN SCHOOL PUPILS (In Percent Responding)

American Sample[a]

Professionalization of Attitude by Grade Level for Males (N—472)

Grade Level	N	1-2 (play)	3-4 Scale Score	5-6 (success)	Total
3	(83)	78.2	12.1	9.7	100.0
6	(94)	72.4	20.2	7.4	100.0
8	(76)	31.6	52.6	15.8	100.0
10	(131)	28.2	48.1	23.7	100.0
12	(88)	19.3	58.0	22.7	100.0

Canadian Sample[b]

Professionalization of Attitude by Sex (N=564) (Grades 8-12)

Sex	N	1-2 (play)	3-4 Scale Score	5-6 (success)	Total
Male	300	29.01	59.26	11.73	100.0
Female	264	40.53	56.82	2.65	100.0

[a]SOURCE: Webb, 1969, p. 170.

[b]SOURCE: Maloney and Petrie, 1972, p. 184.

with 60 nonparticipants. Both samples were comprised of eleven year old boys from middle class families living in a northern suburb of Washington, D.C. On the basis of Webb's scale which was administered to each subject they found that participants in organized sport considered skill or victory as the most important factor in play while nonparticipants stressed the factor of fairness.

Perhaps competitive children in Maloney and Petrie's and Mantel and VanderVelden's samples are being well-socialized for more adult competitive roles in athletics. Their findings regarding the professionalization of attitudes toward play among competitive preadolescents closely parallel attitudes toward sportsmanship among college students reported by Richardson (1962). He administered the Haskins and Hartmen's Action-Choice Tests for Competitive Sport Situations to 233 senior male physical education majors at 15 institutions and found that: (1) "non-letter winners indicated a higher degree of sportsmanship than did letter winners," (2) "those students receiving no athletic grants scored much higher than respondents receiving athletic grants," and (3) "football players ranked below all other sports in test scores." These findings suggest that to the adage "nice guys finish last" one should add the clause "among young and old alike."

Concluding Remarks

In the course of my brief but broad survey of physical activity patterns of Canadians and Americans at various age levels, I hope that I have added fuel to the fire of the hot issue at hand: "Sport for adults, athletics for children." Needless to say, I am most concerned with the daily duffer at all age levels where performance doesn't count, but participation does. That is to say, if sports are worth playing, they are worth playing badly. Therefore, it is rather disheartening to see that sport participation is largely limited to young males, with mature adults of either sex and females of all ages being nearly totally disenfranchised from sport participation. I am also personally dismayed that participation in active sports by young and old alike is restricted to such a limited number of agonetic activities.

By way of conclusion I would like to raise the question of: "What does the future hold?" On the one hand, many would argue that the picture of participation which I have painted is rapidly changing for the better. These optimists could cite the profound changes which might occur in the case of women's involvement in sport as the result of recent legislation regarding equal rights for women in athletic activities at all levels from professional tennis to Little League baseball. They could cite recent studies which show changing attitudes toward competition and success (see e.g., Looney, 1973; "Survey Finds Views Change on Success"). They could also argue that a leisure ethic is replacing the work ethic (cf. Sutton, 1973). And they might even make a strong case that the current energy crisis in North America will break-up the present five-day work pattern and markedly change our leisure life-styles (cf., Safire, 1973). I personally believe that these trends as well as many other social trends characteristic of our coming post-industrial society (cf., Bell, 1973) auger well for social change in the realm of sport.

On the other hand as I am a pessimist by nature, I suggest that change is likely to occur at a much slower pace than that envisioned by the optimists. For example, Robinson has compared time-budget data collected by Lundberg *et. al.* in the 1930's with that collected by Converse and Robinson in the mid-1960's. Robinson (1969) states that ". . . it would appear that leisure time (about five hours per day on the average) has not increased markedly over the last 35 years" (p. 75); moreover, he specifically shows that men and women spent fewer minutes of their leisure time on sport activities in 1965-66 than adults in 1934 (p. 76). Staffan B. Linder (1970) in an elegant little treatise titled *The Harried Leisure Class* argues on socio-economic grounds that we can expect a greater scarcity of time in the immediate future and an even more hectic tempo of life-style. He makes a persuasive case that even if our non-work time increases leisure time will not.

A glimpse of the slow social change in sport situations can be readily gleaned from a historical comparison of annual national survey polls. Table 17 compares primary and secondary sport involvement patterns of American adults for the years 1959 and 1973. Figures in the table indicate that at best only moderate change has taken place in basic sport participation patterns. Finally, I present for your consideration Table 18 which shows comparative growth patterns for disposable personal income, total recreational spending, and sporting good sales. The data nicely confirms Parkinson's Second Law that "expenditures rise to meet income." The data also support a corollary to Parkinson's Law that: "Leisure expenditures rise to meet disposable personal income"; or expressed more specifically, "expenditures for recreational resources is a constant function of the amount of discretionary income" (hereafter known as Loy's Law #1). Having brought some law and order to bear upon the North American syndrome, let me give the platform to our next panelist whom I am sure will raise havoc.

Table 17

A HISTORICAL COMPARISON OF GALLUP POLL SURVEYS
OF THE SPORT INVOLVEMENT OF AMERICAN ADULTS[a]

"Which of these sports and activities have you participated in within the past 12 months?"

Sport	1959	1973
1. Swimming	33%	42%
2. Bowling	18	28
3. Fishing	32	24
4. Baseball/softball	11	19
5. Hunting	16	14
6. Golf	8	14
7. Tennis	4	12

"Which of these sports have you attended at *least once* during the last 12 months?"

Sport	1959	1973
1. Football	23	33
2. Baseball	28	30

3. Basketball	18	23
4. Boxing	4	14
5. Soccer	1	13
6. Horse Racing	9	10
7. Wrestling	6	7
8. Hockey	4	7
9. Track & Field	2	6
10. Dog Racing	2	4
11. Tennis	2	2
12. Stock Car Racing	9	2

ªSOURCE: *Gallup Opinion Index* (Feb. 1973), Report 92, pp. 24-27.

Table 18

COMPARATIVE GROWTH PATTERNS: DISPOSABLE PERSONAL
INCOME, TOTAL RECREATIONAL SPENDING, AND
SPORTING GOODS SALES

Year	Disposable Personal Income	Year-to-Year Percentages of Change		
		D.P.I.	Total Rec.*	SG Sales**
1948	$189,300,000,000	+11.3	+ 4.9	+ 5.9
1949	189,654,000,000	+ 0.2	+ 3.2	— 1.0
1950	207,655,000,000	+ 9.5	+11.4	+ 8.3
1951	227,481,000,000	+ 9.5	+ 3.8	+ 5.8
1952	238,714,000,000	+ 4.9	+ 4.7	+ 7.3
1953	252,474,000,000	+ 5.8	+ 5.2	+ 6.7
1954	256,885,000,000	+ 1.7	+ 2.8	+ 0.5
1955	274,448,000,000	+ 6.8	+ 7.3	+ 7.4
1956	292,942,000,000	+ 6.7	+ 6.8	+ 7.2
1957	308,791,000,000	+ 5.4	+ 5.9	+ 6.4
1958	317,924,000,000	+ 3.0	+ 4.7	+ 4.0
1959	337,145,000,000	+ 6.0	+ 8.7	+ 7.6
1960	349,889,000,000	+ 3.8	+ 6.6	+ 8.9
1961	364,684,000,000	+ 4.2	+ 5.3	+ 4.4
1962	384,558,000,000	+ 5.4	+ 4.6	+ 6.6
1963	402,472,000,000	+ 4.7	+ 5.6	+ 5.3
1948-63	431,852,000,000p	+ 7.3	+ 5.7	+ 5.7

* Total Recreation Expenditures
**Sporting Goods Expenditures
SOURCE: Snyder, 1965, Table 2c.

AAHPER, "Desirable Athletic Competition for Children of Elementary School Age," Washington, D.C.: American Association for Health, Physical Education, and Recreation, 1968.

Alderman, Richard B., "A Sociopsychological Assessment of Attitude Toward Physical Activity in Champion Athletes," *Research Quarterly* 41 (March 1970), pp. 1-9.

Bell, Daniel, *The Coming of Post-Industrial Society*, New York: Basic Books, Inc., 1973.

Curtis, James E., and Brian G. Milton, "Social Status and the Sedentary Society: National Data on Leisure-Time Physical and Sports Activities in Canada," Paper presented at the annual meetings of the Southern Sociological Society, Atlanta, Georgia, April 13, 1973.

Ferriss, Abbot L., (editor and project director) *National Recreation Survey* (Outdoor Recreation Review Commission Study Report No. 19), Washington, D.C. U.S. Government Printing Office, 1962.

"Few and Far Between," *Sports Illustrated* (Sept. 24, 1973), p. 22.

Gallup Opinion Index (Feb. 1973), Report 92.

Kenyon, Gerald S., "The Significance of Physical Activity as a Function of Age, Sex Education, and Socio-Economic Status of Northern United States Adults," *International Review of Sport Sociology* 1 (1966), pp. 41-57.

Linder, Staffan B., *The Harried Leisure Class*. New York: Columbia University Press, 1970.

Looney, Douglas S., "Why Grab A Brass Ring?" *The National Observer* 12 (July 21, 1973), pp. 1-23.

Maloney, T. Lawrence, and Brian M. Petrie, "Professionalization of Attitude Toward Play Among Canadian School Pupils as a Function of Sex, Grade and Athletic Participation," *Journal of Leisure Research* 4 (Summer 1972), pp. 184-195.

Mantel, Richard, and Lee Vander Velden, "The Relationship Between the Professionalization of Attitude Toward Play of Pre-adolescent Boys and Participation in Organized Sports," Paper presented at the Third International Symposium on the Sociology of Sport, Waterloo, Ontario, Canada, August 22-28, 1971.

Milton, Brian G., "Sport and Social Stratification: Correlates of Sport Involvement in the Canadian Context," Paper presented at First Canadian Congress of Sport and Physical Activity, Montreal, Quebec, October 14, 1973.

National Collegiate Athletic Association, "The Sports and Recreational Programs of the Nation's Universities and Colleges," (Report No. 3) Kansas City, Missouri: NCAA, 1968.

Petrie, Brian M., "Achievement Orientations in Adolescent Attitudes Toward Play," *International Review of Sport Sociology* 6 (1971), pp. 89-99.

Rarick, G. Lawrence, "Competitive Sports in Childhood and Early Adolescence," Chapter 14, pp. 364-386, In a Lawrence Rarick (ed.), *Physical Activity, Human Growth and Development*. New York: Academic Press, 1973.

Richardson, Dean E., "Ethical Conduct in Sport Situations," *Proceedings of the Annual Meeting of The National College Physical Education Association For Men,"* 66 (December 1962), pp. 98-104.

Robinson, John P., "Social Change as Measured by Time Budgets," *Journal of Leisure Research* 1 (Winter 1969), pp. 75-77.

Robinson, John P., "Daily Participation in Sport Across Twelve Countries," pp. 156-173, In Gunther Luschen (editor), *The Cross-Cultural Analysis of Sport and Games*. Champaign, Illinois: Stipes Publishing Company, 1970.

Safire, William, "Four-Day Week," *New York Times,* November 22, 1973, p. 37.

Sillitoe, K. K., *Planning for Leisure*. London: Her Majesty's Stationery Office, 1969.

Snyder, Richard, *Trends in the Sporting Goods Market: 1947-65*. Chicago, Ill.: National Sporting Goods Association, 1965.

Stone, Gregory P., "American Sports — Play and Display," *Chicago Review* 9 (Fall 1955), pp. 83-100.

"Survey Finds Views Change on Success," *New York Times,* November 1, 1973, p. 37.

Sutton, Horace, "The Leisure Ethic," *World* (June 5, 1973), p. 42.

Webb, Harry, "Professionalization of Attitudes Toward Play Among Adolescents," Chapter 8, pp. 161-187, In Gerald S. Kenyon (ed.), *Aspects of Contemporary Sport Sociology*. Chicago: Athletic Institute, 1969.

Cecil Eaves
Development Coordinator
Amateur Sports, CAHA

I have always been in a fortunate position to have a captive audience like we have here today. I don't know if most of you have had some teaching experience to any extent. Maybe you were like me and had the last class of the day, and you didn't know how to get their attention. I have been in that position on a number of occasions and I have had to use various ways and means. However, one of the best ways I came across was a result of a car ride that my wife and I were taking one Sunday. We were listening to the CBC radio program and the announcer was asking people across Canada to phone in their favorite joke and it wasn't very funny. One woman phoned and said, "Well, I have a joke that my husband tells, would you mind if I tell you on the phone?" and he said, "Sure, go ahead."

So, she said to him "How do you call a deaf duck?"
You could just hear the guy on the phone, you know the wheels are going round.

And, finally, he said, "How do you call a deaf duck?" Yelling: "Hey duck!"

And, now that I have your attention.

The first time that I told that was in my anatomy class with one hundred and five students and this girl was writing and when I told that she jumped about a foot out of her chair.

So, in a democracy, "Sport For Adults," "Athletics For Children," is probably going to be with us for some time. The thing that maybe we can do as concerned people in society, is provide some insight to parents, to coaches, and to adults about what types of things that they might be doing from a very practical point in guiding their child through sport or athletics or whatever term you would like to use.

As a representative of the Canadian Amateur Hockey Association, I would like to outline a number of procedures that the organization is attempting to do in order to re-focus on our approach to the teaching and coaching of minor hockey in Canada.

Hockey has contributed as much as any sport to this sports/athletics syndrome, and you have to ask the question why? I think that part of the answer can be supplied by a little story that was passed on to me two weeks ago. I had occasion to come back to Windsor and I drove into Michigan to give a talk at a hockey clinic, and I came across a friend who had just recently started to coach in the International Hockey League. He said to me: "You know, Cec, one of the things that really bothered me at the beginning of the season was having to tell the fellows who weren't good enough to make the club. I got it down to the last ten and I brought them in, talked with them and told them. I got the biggest shock of my life, because each of them thanked me for asking him to leave the team." And, he said, "Why do you thank me?" The fellow answered, "You are the first person in my life who has told me that I am not good enough to play on a hockey team. I have had hockey stuffed down my throat ever since I was eight years old, and you're the only person that has opened the kind of prison doors that I have been behind, and now I am going to do some of the things that I want to do in my lifetime for the first time. Some of the little things that I have always dreamed about, but I have been so tied to hockey that I haven't been able to do them. Now you have permitted me to do this."

Alright why? Why have parents subjected their kids to this type of environment? I think sociologists and psychologists will indicate to you that everything that we do is based upon a need, and I am here because of a need. We are needy in some way, shape or form and if you take Mazlow's needs or anybody else who has written on needs you usually find that they are composite needs. We have a need to survive, we have a need to make money, we have a need to romance, and this can be broken down in terms of sex, future, promise, new experience, and there is a need for recognition, and then Mazlow's last need, for self-actualization. I think all of us in some way strive for self-actualization. It has been my experience with people in sport, and in particular hockey, that vicariously they try to self-actualize. They get to the point through their son, that they were never able to reach themselves. This is self-actualization for them, to the extent that if you draw these other points in, that there is the new experience. Many parents become directors of their kids. They are directing them here and they are directing them there, they bring in the future promise, oftentimes this is not done consciously but subconsciously.

The average salary in the National Hockey League today is $50,000. and that is an awful lot of money. Parents say "My son is going to make it to the National Hockey League come hell or high water, and I am going to push him and I am going to drive him until he gets there. Because then, maybe not only will my son become recognized as a great hockey player, but I also will become recognized as the father of that boy, and in part, I become self-actualized." The thing that I ask is at what price do kids have to pay in order to maybe help the parents self-actualize? Are the needs of the kids being met? Because there is such a concern for the needs of children in this country, last October under the advice of the government, the Canadian Hockey Association in conjunction with the Hockey Canada, got together and formed a Hockey Technical Advisory Committee. Now this committee is concerned with the development of hockey in the country, not only from a physical point of view, but also from a psychological point of view.

What insights can we provide parents in this country about their children participating in sport? At a national hockey planning seminar that was held in Scarboro on September 9th to 12th, we had a philosophy session. It became quite apparent from this session that really we should have spent all three days just talking about philosophy, because we know an awful lot about what goes into the make up of a hockey player, but we don't really know what the psychological implications are. And, I am sure that this Hockey Technical Advisory Committee is going to look very favorably in the future on having a Seminar devoted strictly to philosophy, and how we can communicate with the coaches and the parents of this country.

Now, in addition to that as a result of the symposium in Kingston on the child in sport and physical activity the hockey technical advisory committee and I should say their research committee, is looking into their competitive hockey for boys under ten. Now, we don't know whether this is good or bad, but we would like to find out. Any of you who go to an arena and watch the way that parents react, maybe, you have the same impression that I do. That really this competitive sport is not really that good, but we really don't know. We can theorize, but this research subcommittee is going to look into this and see if we can come up with some answers that we can communicate with the public.

From a personal point of view, and this is not a sales commercial, I have had the good fortune of working on a book entitled

Let's Play Better Hockey with Ken Dryden and John McFarlen. It was produced in co-operation with Hockey Canada and MacDonald's. Ken wrote the introduction and the lead in each chapter, and John and I along with many other people in Canada had a great deal to do with the content of each chapter. Now, MacDonald's felt so highly of this book that they put half-a-million dollars into the production of it. During minor hockey week which is being run by the Canadian Amateur Hockey Association on January the 19th to the 26th, we are also going to sell this book. And, maybe we can communicate this message about a philosophical approach to the game. We don't know how successful we are going to be, we have to make some overtures to the Canadian public. This is not a how-to-do-it book, but it asks a few basic questions, and I think the book can be pretty well summarized by a letter that Lloyd Percival has put together on the last page. I would like your indulgence to read this letter. We really think that it is the type of letter that each and every parent and coach in Canada should read and take to heart. But, many of them, of course, become so ego-involved that they will read it and say, well, that is fine. But, this is the letter.

Dear Mom and Dad:

I hope that you won't get mad at me for writing this letter, but you always told me never to keep anything back that ought to be brought out into the open. So here goes.

Remember the other morning when my team was playing and both of you were sitting, watching. Well, I hope that you won't get mad at me, but you kind of embarrassed me. Remember when I went after the puck in front of the net trying to score and fell? I could hear you yelling at the goalie for getting in my way and tripping me. It wasn't his fault, that is what he is supposed to do. Then do you remember yelling at me to get on the other side of the blue line. The coach told me to cover my man, and I couldn't if I listened to you, and while I tried to decide they scored against us. Then you yelled at me for being in the wrong place. But, what really got me was what happened after the game. You shouldn't have jumped all over the coach for pulling me off the ice. He is a pretty good coach, and a good guy, and he knows what he is doing. Besides he is just a volunteer coming down at all hours of the day helping us kids, just because he loves sports. And, then neither of you spoke to me the whole way home, I guess you were pretty sore at me for not getting a goal. I tried awfully hard, but I guess I am a crummy hockey player. But, I love the game, it is lots of fun being with the other kids and learning to compete. It is a good sport, but how can I learn if you don't show me a good example. And, anyhow I thought I was playing hockey for fun, to have a good time and like to learn good sportsmanship. I didn't know that you were going to get so upset, because I couldn't become a star.

Love,
Your son.

Lloyd Percival and his wife have put together ten points. I am not going to read all ten, but two of them are appropriate. Their point about a parent relationship to their child is: "Be helpful but don't coach your son on the way to the game or at the breakfast table." How many of us have had that happen to us? You didn't do this last night, you didn't do that, you should have got five goals. Think how tough it is on him to be continually innundated with advice, pep talks and criticisms. And, the other point, and maybe you can recognize something here. I chose this point because I have three sons which I just about ruined when they were younger for this very reason: "Try not to live your life through your son." You have lost as well as won, you have been frightened, you have backed off at times, you have been the villain. Don't expect any better of him. Sure he is an extension of you, but don't assume that he feels the same way that you do, wants the same things, or has the same attitudes. Don't push him in the direction that will give you the most satisfaction.

Now all this is geared maybe to helping parents understand that the child has a need that should be met. There is this self-actualization which needs to be met. But, self-actualization can be met with guidance. The guidance we are trying to provide in Canada is one whereby the Canadian Amateur Hockey Association has appointed, in each branch, technical directors and hopefully in a year or two we are going to have permanent people. Right now in the eleven CAHA branches we only have four permanent people. If we can get these individuals going across the country talking about philosophy, then maybe this message can be communicated to parents and coaches. The CAHA has recently taken another step in that we have hired, as of last Thursday, Mr. Murray Costello, who many of you know. Murray is a former professional hockey player, and has been very involved with public relations and promotion work in the United States. Now, in addition, we would hope that as these eleven technical directors go across the country, assisted by Murray, that they strongly emphasize two books that are on the market. One is Dr. Thomas Harris' book *I'm O.K., You're O.K.* and the other book that all coaches should read *They Call Me Coach* by Luden.

As a result of ten years' work with handicapped children I developed a three point credo that I have tried to follow with each and every team that I have coached and with my own family. The points are:

You need to establish standards for the age group that you are working with, and this involves your going and doing a little research and finding out just what kids at nine and ten years of age need. I have had some rather interesting stories related to me about people, coaches, and parents. Not really understanding what their kids are all about at nine or ten years of age. An example of this concerned a fellow in Ottawa. He went into the dressing room and here were a group of nine year old boys, and they were ready to go out on the ice and their mouth pieces were in and this is the way that they were sitting. Now is that typical of a group of nine year olds. And that is really kind of sad, because we make little robots out of these kids, because we impose our adult values on them. To recapitulate, establish standards for the age group that you are working with, and then communicate these standards with the kids. Sit down with them and ask them what they want out of sports. Now, maybe this is idealistic, I don't know, but, by golly, it's worth a try, in view of what we are faced with in this country. Secondly, after you have communicated you have to recognize that there is a need to be consistent with the player who is the best on your team, and the player who has the least ability and in order to be consistent you have to develop strategy. Now, if any of us here were with each other because we are all unique individuals we would have to develop a strategy in order to meet each of our needs and that's the important thing.

And, then the third thing is to create an environment where kids can grow and develop, and that takes a lot of doing.

In conclusion, this amounts to the fact that we are trying to do right here, create an environment of understanding, so that in the final analysis the needs of the kids are being met, in addition to the needs of the parent.

Discussion Period

Question

The main problem with the kids fourteen through eighteen is their names are on the court lists too often because there is nothing to do. Is there any way that the pyramid can be squeezed at the bottom to make it more acceptable for the age group at the top?

DR. EAVES

Well there probably is, but you're working against a system that is basically oriented to professional hockey. We really don't have too many alternatives in Canada other than professional hockey. Father David Bauer attempted in the early sixties to provide an alternative, but this only lasted for a period of five or six years. We have attempted to provide in our colleges another alternative by having a student national team, but this has not proved successful today. Also, by the time a young man reaches the age of thirteen or fourteen, he has been pretty well processed through the machine and he knows whether or not he is going to become a professional hockey player. This is kind of sad, somewhere in the communities we have to straighten away our values, and provide time for these kids to *play*. But, there is a lack of ice facilities. It is very possible that we could work this into the school system in some way, but by and large the school system has been very reticent to get involved in this.

It's interesting from a comparative point of view to take a look at where the emphasis is placed in Russia, and where the emphasis is placed in the United States, or where the emphasis is placed in Canada. For example, Russia has a whole club system. A boy can get involved in community hockey. They call it their backyard program in Moscow, and if he is good enough to evolve into a club team then he can play for one of six teams, Red Army, Spartak, etc. They still have a broad base, but they have a channel right up the middle, which is their club system, and that is a bit different than ours. In order to coach a club team you have to be a qualified hockey coach, and you are required to have spent four years at a physical culture institute in Moscow. Now these physical culture institutes specialize in the preparation of coaches. There are twenty-three of them in the Soviet Union and seven of them zero in on ice hockey, that happens to be their specialty. The one in Moscow that we visited, that was their special area.

In the United States, of course, you have the whole system geared to the schools and to the university. So this is where their athletes come from.

In Canada, we have taken hockey out of the schools. We did this many years ago. The communities, and the volunteer coaches are providing the leadership. This is where we are concerned as a Hockey Technical Advisory Committee, about educating as best as we can the parents and the coaches. So that maybe the values change a little bit and the boy in the age group of fourteen, fifteen, and sixteen can see some reason for staying and playing.

Question

I want to know why was there more time spent by society on sports in the thirties, was the society geared for sport rather than athletics?

Dr. Loy

When I say there was more time it was like eight minutes per day instead of five. So in terms of the amount of free time, the amount of free times remain about the same, and the percent of that free time spent on sports has not changed a great deal. These studies were both done on the east coast so it does not reflect the United States as a whole, but it doesn't seem to be much changed. I think what has occurred is that TV has certainly changed the world in terms of spectatorship. There may well be more of our free time invested in sport through TV than there was, say, in the thirties. I think what has occurred is we may have one or two more hours of non-work time. The change has not been much, but we have gone from perhaps a forty hour week to a thirty-six hour week in certain professions. So there is a few more minutes per day for all adults in terms of non-work, but most of this non-work time is not free time as we have to eat, and we have to sleep, we have to maintain ourselves. And, all of the goods we have today that were to give us greater free time, we spend most of our time maintaining those goods. So many friends of mine will drive an hour to two hours to and from work.

I was at a city college in New York this week, and everyone that I met there on the staff drove at least a half hour and most of them drove up to two hours to and from work. Well, this is not work time, but it's not free, free time if you will.

And, the same thing would be true of trying to maintain our cars and TV set and so on. There are all sorts of things that we do expending time and our non-work time that is not what we call free time. Therefore, we don't have any time to invest in sport or games or whatever it might be. The best source of this is a book by Stephan Linder, who is a professor in Sweden and who studied in the United States. He has a book that is out in paper back now, as well as hard back, entitled *The Harried Leisure Class* and he makes a very thorough and sophisticated case. To the extent that time is just as scarce now as it was forty years ago, and it is going to remain scarce, and then our free time is going to remain fairly constant for the next twenty or thirty years. Notwithstanding the fact that we may not work as much on the job.

Question

Can anything be done in the NHL to clean up the bush league attitude that they have towards the officials? I am referring to the swearing that you see after the guy receives the penalty for bumping into the referee, and you can see this filtrating into the minor hockey.

Dr. Eaves

Well, I think this goes back to the Hockey Technical Advisory Committee on what we are trying to do in terms of establishing an identity for minor hockey, and establishing values that are appropriate for the youngsters that are playing the game. Now it is going to be very hard to overcome this because the mass media through Hockey Night in Canada has a monopoly on that, but through the efforts of Hockey Canada, hopefully we can get some programs on what values should be transmitted for the young player, which are over and above what we see the professional exhibiting. There is a development committee in Canada, and this development committee is thinking very seriously of forming subcommittees which concentrate on violence and the legal rights of players. I don't know what the results are going to be but it would at least be an initial step by this subcommittee to take a look at violence in hockey and maybe come up with some recommendations. Then also, we need some information for young players as to the legal rights, and we actually need information from the professionals on what their legal rights are.

Interjection

I think one thing that could be done like you can see one official will give you ten if you mouth off and the other official will just turn away. But, if the official will give you ten right away, I think that would clean it up a lot.

Answer

I guess it depends on how the official reads the tempo of the game and that would be a National Hockey League problem. I don't know how much influence we can have, we are going to attempt to have as best as we can to have an influence, but you have an entertainment business in the professionals.

Question

Personally yesterday because of the concerted attack upon athletics I found myself playing the role of an advocate of athletics, and I do believe that there are certain values attached to athletics. I define athletics as a physical contest in which the primary purpose of the participant is to demonstrate his excellence according to agreed upon rules in a contest. And, winning really is the name of the game now, not winning at all costs. It is a very very bad thing where Lombardi supposedly says that winning it is the only thing. Actually if you go back and look at a 1954 edition of *Sports Illustrated* you will find that Jim Tadum made that statement when he was at North Carolina and Lombardi was an unknown at Army at the time as an assistant coach.

My fundamental point is basically this, that play is a wonderful thing and here in Canada apparently you have the same problems that we do in the United States with regards to, say, baseball. Little league baseball becomes an agonistic athletic contest for many people, and many parents attempt to live through their children with regards to the achievements that they might make. If we could, if it were possible to get people in the schools that understood and recognize the values of playful activities as such, we could learn a certain amount of skills, we could have a good time, and we could prepare the way for those people who are competitive by nature and who seek voluntarily to demonstrate their excellence in contests, which I regard as athletics. Until people stop confusing terminology and until people stop talking about the Chicago Bears playing the Kansas City Chiefs or the Daltons playing whatever you want. Until we stop talking about play in a sense, it is really not play at all. We actually cheat ourselves by failing to recognize that there is a type of human activity in which maximizing the joy of the contest is very very important and our schools should, particularly, maybe in Physical Education, make an attempt to turn out people who have a real appreciation for the value of play, for the job of the moment, for maximizing the pleasure of the moment, for teaching skills in a non-competitive way, and at the same time, embracing the fact that there are certain people who are going to be highly competitive who are going to want to test their ability against others.

My point in summation is that it would be a very very good thing to have a whole new sort of re-education on the values of play and to introduce young people to activities which really are games to be played but can become if you so wish agonistic contests in which you can demonstrate your excellence. And, I would like to have the panelists particularly John Loy's comments on that long talk.

DR. LOY

I think you have hit on something that I would like to see done in a grade school setting. I am not opposed to athletics for young boys or girls, if in fact they have a choice and if in fact they know what is in athletics or what is in play. They never really have the contrast to compare the two. I think it would be fun to take a little league baseball team and have them play for a month in the athletic sense, and define what you meant by athletics and have them involved in very intense competition. Then take that same team and have them play baseball the next month in the form of play. If you can define what you meant by that. Then let them think through the two in terms of what they receive and what they didn't receive. What they liked about each, what they disliked about each. I guess this is the only thing that disturbs me is that through all ranks of life one has so little choice as to how he must engage. So very few students, college or high school students, have a chance to engage in athletics if indeed they wanted to. Likewise many that would like to engage and play sport forms have little chance. You know we just don't entertain that idea at all.

Question

The first question revolves around this problem of competition and play, and I think that we can pretty safely state that the more formalized you make the competition for the game itself the more important winning becomes. And, my question, therefore, is if we want our youngsters to learn to play so to speak, should we not eliminate formalized competition? And, if we should to what age should we prohibit formalized competition?

DR. EAVES

How do you do that in a democracy? They found out in their study at the University of Windsor that by and large people don't even have any objectives for these associations. They are just going out there and it's competition for competition sake, let's get the kids out on the field, let's get them playing or let's get them out on the ice, drop the puck, and so they really don't know what it's all about.

Question

Really it is a personal concern as I have a ten year old boy who is on a soccer team. The team went to a Western Canadian championship and I was the only parent on the entire team opposed to the youngster playing even outside the city at ten years of age, and what has he got left once he goes beyond that kind of thing. And, I know that the youngster underwent certain pressures while he was away which I felt were not all that healthy, and yet we were the only parents who were against it. What are you going to do, are you going to take the kid out of the situation? Now what responsibility does the sports association have for sponsoring these kinds of things? I appreciate your comments relative to these organizations that kick the money in to support these events. Maybe they could direct it to older kids. Groups where the individual is supposedly emotionally and psychologically mature enough to be able to resist the adult pressures that we put on them it might be more appropriate. But, what is the CAHA doing in terms of controlling organized competition for five and six year olds, which we see happening?

Dr. Eaves

I go back to my comment about how do you do that in a democracy? You have to recognize that the CAHA is the regulatory body of hockey in the country, and that each provincial association is autonomous unto themselves and then it goes down to the Riverside Association and say the Windsor Hockey Association. This is what makes it tough and that is why Change Agent Research is so important. It isn't the associations in themselves, it isn't the CAHA that starts these kids playing at age five and six, it's the parents. They form these leagues for their kids four, five, six and seven and the associations, say in Riverside, sees what kind of leadership they are getting from the parents and boy. It's ram it in and let's go boys, grab the puck and drop it and scrimmage seventy games.

I coached a Pee Wee team last year here in Windsor and some of the American teams played as many as a hundred and forty games. And, we ask why the kids are fed up with hockey at fifteen and sixteen. With the Pee Wee team last year we played sixty-one games and that was an absolute minimum and I had to really struggle to keep it to sixty-one games. So, it's the associations taking the parents under their wing and providing them some framework. Now as a CAHA or as the Ontario Hockey Association or Ontario Minor Hockey Association, I don't know that we have the right to come in and impose this on the parents in a democracy. Now I could be all wrong, but maybe it serves something like Change Agent Research where people are being provided with some insight as to what is happening to these kids. That is why this research study of the Hockey Technical Advisory Committee is so important. But, it has to be done over a long range because we have to come up with some answers. John and Jerry Kenyon and the people who work in sociology of sport they are going to have to supply us with some theoretical base so that maybe we in the working of the practical end can take some of their theory and implement it. Jim Duthie and Dick Moriarty have got it down to a practical approach also, but we need the theory, we need to blend both of them, but it is tough in a democracy; boy, it's easy in Russia. It's darn easy, and the interesting thing is, of course, Russia reminds me very much of where we were in the 1940's. Where did most of the great hockey players come from in the National League in the 1940's, and 1950's? It was from the west. And, why did they come from the west? Because of the depression, and it was a means of social mobility for them. It is the same thing in the Soviet Union, if you are an athlete of any note, say a hockey player or a basketball player it can mean the difference between your sharing with five families one bathroom or having a bathroom of your own. It means that maybe you can drive in your own car. It is easy in the Soviet Union, because they have more leisure time, for guardians to get on the Metro and spend an hour taking their nephew and their grandson down to the Red Army to be there at six o'clock in the morning for a practice. Now that is part of their society. I don't know if we can do that in our society, in a democracy.

Question

My concern really is, as a university coach. I find a lot of our athletes that come up to the university are hung up on winning and losing, and they choke, simply because when the pressure gets a little tough they start thinking "Oh, I might lose," instead of putting out the fullest effort.

Interjection

I appreciate what you say about your own son being involved in this travelling bit and that is one of the things that really gets to me. I can remember reading where these little leaguers from Japan came over to Pennsylvania and won the world's championship. Ten year olds. What is left in life?

Question

I was reading in the Manitoba paper on the way here about an O'Keefe Grant for a coaching development program for hockey, and it indicated that the individuals will get Level I, and Level II, and Level III coaching certification. Level I amounted to a three hour session. Level II, I think was a one day thing, and Level III, was a two-and-a-half day seminar.

I wonder whether this is sufficient qualification for coaches to really understand and know something about it.

DR. EAVES

Quite frankly no. The thing that we have to do is get the people warm and get them exposed in a three hour session. Eighty percent of our coaches in Canada are at Level I and II. They are the volunteer father, the concerned father, there is nobody to coach the boys' team so we want to give them a minimal exposure just get them warm to find out what it is all about. In Canada it isn't enough to put the kids on the ice, drop the puck and have them go to it. There is a strange phenomena here, and it relates to the fact that many of us just view hockey that way. When you get to the top you sometimes forget all the little things that you had to do in order to achieve the plateau, and that is what has happened to us in Canadian hockey. We have had in this country since 1950 the most complete and concise book that has ever been written, and it was written by Lloyd Percival in 1950. But, very few of us bother to delve through this, but the Russians did, the Czechs did. As a matter of fact, I think that Terrisof copyrighted Percival's book and published it in Moscow. And, the thing is that they study the game, they broke it down, not only physically, but mentally and psychologically, so that they know what all the parts are. The thing that we noticed the most in the Soviet Union was regarding young kids. They enjoyed working with their instructor, they enjoyed playing hockey. The fellow who was their coach had gone through the physical culture institute, and had played on the national team and also his mentality was geared to seven and eight year old boys and he was quite happy and content working with these young fellows.

So, what we have to do, in summation, is get the people exposed to Levels I and II. Get them to realize that there is more to hockey than just dropping the puck. There is a heck of a lot of parts, and somewhere we have to take a hold and break the parts down so that they understand what goes into the game. We have done this for years in football and basketball and for some unknown reason we haven't done this in hockey.

Question

I wanted to talk about this Change Agent Research. Dr. Loy suggested that we take the same group that played sports and then try them in something in athletics or vice versa. Well, we may have this chance to study it after this year here. The changes that came about after the project last winter here at Windsor are that they are now playing two teams sideways in the rink and all this year there will be no score, and no standing in the Pee Wee Hockey League. They are going to measure whether or not this is satisfactory, and will it change the philosophies and I wonder? They say the only noticeable change so far (because it just began this month) is that the parents are all sitting together on one side, rather than as opponents sitting on either side of the rink and paying more attention to their coffee than they are to the hockey because they are up at six in the morning. The pressure's off, there is no score. The parents don't have to be there yelling at the kids loudly. I wonder, Dr. Eaves, if this thing is good. If after the end of this year they find out that it is not important, where does that leave the kids for learning their skills if this thing is found to be good.

DR. EAVES

Hopefully we can get some kind of structure started in Canada whereby we would have key people across the country. It would possibly go to various communities and help them take a look at themselves. I am most interested to see what happens but the ego involvement isn't there, of course, in just what you said. Maybe it is, but not at the degree that it was.

Question

I have been involved in hockey a little bit and I am concerned about one thing in hockey that you haven't said anything about, and I think that it applies to all sports and all athletics, and that is I believe that there are many components. One component happens to be the rules and I haven't heard anyone say anything about referees and I haven't heard anyone say anything about the fact that a lot of children between the ages of fourteen and eighteen can't afford to play hockey in the atmosphere that the game is played in. I often said to my wife that if my son lived to be four it would be great because he wasn't too well coordinated. Then when he got to be eight I thought that was fine and now that he is ten I think he may be hurt soon. He can do almost anything, and not get hurt, the refereeing doesn't matter at that point, but when they get to be sixteen years of age and they carry a weapon and there are a couple of sports like lacrosse and hockey where we give the guy a weapon and say go and have fun. We don't have any concern for the referees. I don't see the CAHA or anyone getting the attitude of getting referees to the point where they volunteer also.

DR. EAVES

I am glad that you brought that up, because on September 30th there was a national referees' planning seminar and based upon the hockey coaches' planning seminar that we had in Scarborough. I made a presentation to the referees on behalf of the Hockey Technical Advisory Committee to in fact start to develop or look into the development of the referees certification program. Steps are being taken now by various people across the country to supply some information, so that the calibre of the refereeing is enhanced.

One of the interesting things that happened at another clinic that I attended in Saskatchewan was the fact that for the first time in any clinic that I have ever attended the referees and coaches came together. They actually communicated, and it was quite funny. Danny McLeod was talking to the coaches and I had the opportunity to talk to the referees. Dan said, "You know one of the things that has evolved from us referees is the fact that when a hockey game starts there is only three sane people in the arena. That is the referee and the two linesmen," and maybe there is a lot of truth in that. But there are steps being taken in order to upgrade the calibre of refereeing in this country. We are trying to suggest to each and every association that when they have clinics in the future, the referees and coaches get together so that they are not as antagonistic towards each other as they have been in the past.

Comments from the floor

Dr. Eaves, I have never found any lack of communication between a referee and a coach. You might have to use a few bleeps to tell all about it but it's there.

I would like to share something with the panel and the fellow delegates here today. I think we all have interest and concern for what's happening to kids today. I am an elementary school principal and have been involved in coaching for many years. I would like to tell you about a practice that in the last couple of years I have taken on. I am going to allude to something that Dr. Eaves mentioned at the beginning of his presentation this morning. That was about the kid who said for the first time somebody told him he wasn't good enough. I have been practicing low key confrontation, and that's telling coaches to take a look at themselves (either on the telephone or by writing them a letter in a personal way, in a private way) so as not to embarrass them you know, with all these ideas of humanism and so on. I am doing this in a couple of ways and this is no plug but for the last couple of years I have been running a coaching course here in this city of Windsor for the Continuing Education Department of the humanistic approach to handling kids. We publicized it in the papers and it has been on the radio, and in all, two years ago we had twelve coaches apply, and last year we had seventeen. Now, in no way do we stress skills. In fact when they come they say "Are we going to learn about how to throw a ball or something like that?" No. We are going to talk about handling kids, and we brought in a psychologist. We are talking about confronting other coaches and confronting parents. I would like to see every coach write a letter to his parents beforehand and say this is what I believe in, and then live by it. I would like to see us confront coaches.

I would like to relate one experience. I was doing that same function that all school teachers and coaches do and that is exercising the custodial function that we school teachers do. We are glorified baby-sitters, and that is what many of our coaches are, in many ways. We help out the parents that way. Well, I was really baby-sitting my two little boys and I was taking them out for a walk. I saw a Pee Wee Football practice going on. The reason that I was interested in that is because some of the kids in the school where I was principal at that time were out there warming up and I recognized them, and who was controlling this at the beginning of the practice, getting them warmed up, but two young high school kids. I would say they were Grade 11 and 12. The coach had not arrived yet. Alright so the coach had entrusted these two young fellows with the job of warming up the kids. He was going to handle the other stuff, but get them warmed up. This is what I heard and this is what I saw from a distance. Now, right here move your ass over there. Just move it. And, these kids were ten and eleven years of age. You're not going to it. Then they started throwing footballs at the kids.

Now, this happened to be a team that has been in the finals. I happen to know that this team always puts up a good fight and they are always doing well. I noticed then from a distance that as the warm-up finished a car drove up. It was the coach. He walked over and the whole thing changed. O.K. These older kids, these

assistant coaches started patting the kids on the back and everything was great, and the coach took these kids and from a distance
I was impressed at what I saw. The older coach was going through
all the proper motions. I left, I didn't want to embarrass the coach
in front of the kids or get the kids antagonistic. However, I wrote
a letter to the coach when I found out what his name was, and I
told him what was happening. As well, I contacted four of my
parents of these kids and I told them what I had observed, and I
let them follow through from there. I would just like to say that
we have a commitment here. I think that if you really believe that
we should be servicing the kids needs let's get out. It is not easy
I know, but let's get out and tell people in a low key way perhaps
without getting too emotional that maybe there is another way and
maybe they shouldn't be coaching any more.

Question

Dr. Loy has pointed out to us the fact that the pyramid of
participation drops off very rapidly once we pass about age twelve
to thirteen years of age and that in point of fact that by the time a
young man or young woman reaches the age of sixteen or seventeen is spending something like two to five minutes per day on
some form of activity which might be swimming or walking or
something of this nature. We find this not only in parts of the U.S.
where the studies were carried out but we find it in all the cities
across the country. I come from Edmonton, we start with a base of
something like forty thousand young people playing hockey and by
the time we reach age seventeen we are down to about one hockey
team, which must tell us something about the problem of developing enjoyment and fun in this participation thing that we are all
concerned about. It seems to me to a great extent that this relates
directly back to our orientation towards industrialization. We have
to create some kind of an ordered society because they are going to
be involved with the use of machines and machines always require
some form of conformity. If we are going to stress this kind of
conformity on youngsters we are going to create the kind of patho-
logical responses or at least irrational responses that were being
alluded to yesterday by Dr. Keating and so forth.

We almost see this occurring today. A series of studies have
been done where we have shown that competition in fact almost
requires an irrational response on the part of some of our youngsters. A number of studies have been done with the youngsters in

the inner city areas of the U.S. cities where the psychologists have put them into a game situation. The winners would be given some form of reward and the losers would not. They could also cooperate together and one or the other be rewarded for the achievement of a final goal, and these kids would be so competitive that they actually broke fifty pound test ropes trying to get their stick into the goal. Whereas the youngsters from Indian tribes from some parts of Mexico tended to work together to achieve the rewards that were being offered. So this kind of irrational response is being almost inculcated beginning from a very early age. As professionals in this field surely we should be doing something now to protect these kids from this kind of situation. We talked about the kind of protection that we are giving to youngsters and Cec's has said that it is very difficult in a democratic society to protect people like this because the parents want it. The children often think they want it, but we provide a greater degree of security for animals with the SPCA rules than we do for these kids. We get them up in the morning about five and send them down to an ice hockey rink or down to a swimming pool (age class swimming). They come home and have some breakfast and they are off to school again. That evening they are down to a field house or they are down to an arena playing hockey. I was talking to some people in Waterloo who said their son had played five games that week, and he was only nine years old. That's more than the professionals play. Surely somewhere then the question of children's rights must be examined.

The Downey Report in Edmonton has recently pointed out some of the failings that we in our society have not yet met face to face and that is with human rights. Not only from the standpoint of being able to play with the team that they want to play with, but just the sheer fact that we are not considering these young people in any effective way from the standpoint of their need. Psychologists have shown us that the kids in the early formative stages need to be able to assimilate things much more than to accommodate.

Yet, we force them at age five and six into accommodating into a pattern. You know just so you don't get the impression that Windsor has the corner on all the firsts. Edmonton has programs where they play across the rinks with no scoring, with no leagues, etc., we have had it for a couple of years. It seems to be a reasonably effective method, we haven't tested the results of it, but the greatest negative reaction is from the parents. I don't know yet

what we are going to do, but surely, Cec, we have some responsibilities. The people in the Canadian Amateur Hockey Association
have some responsibilities.

The second thing that I think we must look at is the kind of
playing surfaces that they are forcing these young people into at
age ten and eleven. They are playing in soccer at a full scale pitch
with a full size goal. In ice hockey we put these little fellows into
a four by six goal and expect them to be able to cover it or skate
the full length of the ice. It doesn't seem realistic. We put them
into a situation where the adults always have control. In China
they do the other, they put a peer group in positions of control so
that their officials are youngsters their same age and sex.

My question is first of all directed to the academicians, what
kinds of needs do children at different age levels have, different
sexes have, when are we going to get this information out to the
practitioners? And, to the practitioner I say when are we going to
take a stand against the kind of behavior that we currently see
existent that does lead to irrational behavior responses by our
children and say to hell with our democracy right now, these kinds
of things are happening and they are not good?

Answer from the floor

We have made the point that these evils of too much competition and too much strain at an early age exist and I don't think
that you can get away from it. They do exist. Well, that is a very
difficult thing. Cec has indicated that he doesn't know personally.
He doesn't know how you can be effective in creating changes. A
couple of points that I would like to make are that in hockey, for
example, there is desire for change, the fact that the Windsor study
is going on, the fact that it does go on in Edmonton, as a matter of
fact it is not a first for either, because there have been cities across
Canada doing them the last ten years in various ways and various
shapes and forms.

Another point is you have got to change the attitudes, not by
legislation, you have got to change attitudes by providing people
with something with which they can relate which corresponds with
the parents needs, i.e., to make their son a better hockey player.

I know we have a couple of programs which Cec has alluded
to, one called the "beginners' program" which orientated two boys

to an environment which is non-competitive hockey. It's oriented to boys from five to nine years of age. They partake in this and they are going to get as much skilled development as any boy playing in a representative club or in a house league environment. A boy coming through that kind of environment is going to have as much development if not more development than going through a competitive stream.

The point that I am trying to make is that you have to appeal to the hockey team that exists which is I want my Johnny to be a great hockey player to make the $50,000. you have to appeal to their needs and say look Johnny doesn't have to play sixty-one games like Cec's club in order to be a good hockey player. He can play thirty-one games and take another half of his ice time and good practice session and with a good coach and he is going to have better skill development.

I go back to the city of Windsor I don't know the situation, but for example, you know the city of Windsor or whoever controls the ranks is going to say now look, the representative teams have five times as much ice. They don't warrant that, we have to give the house league structure more ice and we have to give them a small competitive thing. If we agree with that we also have to give them developmental ice time in a play situation. The real problem in Ontario is ice civilization.

One essential point that I want to make to the academicians is that you can't legislate change in any environment. You have to appeal to their interest and try to design programs to find methods which brings them in there and notify them over a long period of time.

DR. LOY

For two days about all I have heard is hockey, football and baseball. Now if reflexes were locked into three game forms, pretty much all remarks have been made to men and boys again we are locked into the sex thing. Almost all of our remarks have been on youth, ignoring the dirty old man. Then, in terms of Jerry's remarks about being locked in and meeting needs. These are so fixed at such an early age of five and I expect that they are nearly fixed by age eight. I want to stretch a thing, and all of it applied to sport. On the one hand I'll have to take a stand for male lib, I guess, in the sense that girls, I think in terms of the play, are still permitted to both play with dolls and play with boys or play touch football or whatever it might be. In terms of dress, females can wear pants and so on, but you know the small male child, the boy, early on is so locked into what are male forms of sport that he has a chance to try nothing else but hockey, football, baseball. Has little chance to experiment with anything else, and these are fixed at such an early age. You are speaking of a social change and you are speaking of needs and I am very pessimistic if you accept that sort of thing that these things are well firmed up at an early age and I think Jerry is right but I don't know how to deal with it. I think if we can get off dead center if you think of the two thousand or three thousand games and sport forms that are out there, think of the wide range of different roles that boys and girls try on one or two. I think that this is the sort of thing that has to be experimented with.

Question

Mr. Chairman, I am non-academic, I am a member of the business community that you used to be a member of, the sporting goods business. The tone of the last days in terms of the problems and indeed some real damnation of the competitive sports leaves a concern for me from this point of view. We have twenty-two hundred employees in Canada who are earning their meal ticket by making equipment for baseball, football, lacrosse, hockey, basketball and these dirty competitive sports. Does the panel suggest that with all the problems that we envisage and have been discussing that these sports are going to demise or they are going to be sacrificed in exchange for non-competitive sports, white water, kyaching, sailing, canoeing, and nature hiking and so on, or despite all the problems does the panel still feel that there still will be a retention of the popularity of competitive sports, or indeed some growth?

Dr. Eaves

I am sorry if we have given the impression that competitive sports are to be done away with. In our society we can't do away with them. They are there. It is just a question of how we approach the sports and they're going to exist. It doesn't matter how much we theorize, they are going to be there.

Interjection

I think myself that what we are all talking about is if we are able to change that pyramid to more of a building of a pyramid that you will find a greater expansion.

Question

In spite of Dr. Loy's recent remarks that we are kind of locked in, but in light of some of the information in terms of work done by the University of Windsor could I ask what is the objective of the C.A.H.A.? Have they really examined what they are doing? I have some concern about the announced plans for coaching certification and certification of officials. Because while I see a lot of validity in that approach, the concern that I have is the creation of such a gigantic structure that becomes self-supporting and self-grandizing, that in the end it becomes more important to have more certification of more people of more things when we lose sight of other factors that I would consider more important. Maybe I could generalize it a little further and, Cec could perhaps, I don't want to put you on the spot and certainly I don't know if you can answer on behalf of all the sports governing bodies, but it seems to me that if we go back a little bit and look into our literature there is a very strong recommendation that came out of the American Association and Health Physical Education and Recreation that was endorsed by a joint committee of CAPHER and the American Medical Association that strongly recommended against competition between school teams at the elementary school level. When I look at the development in Canada it seems to me that the sports governing bodies have ignored this completely and through the convenience of organizing competitions outside the schools have disregarded this advice.

Question

The question really comes down to this, "Are the sports governing bodies really assuming their responsibilities?" In light of this information and the knowledge that I think all of us have generally, that competition for younger children is not in their best interest or their wholesome development. What are the sports governing bodies doing to discourage having teams in competition at this level? Children starting at age six, they have played so many games and they have been on so many teams that by the time they are age twelve or thirteen they could not have any interest in that particular activity. Are the sports governing bodies really accepting their responsibility by doing anything that would tend to be interpreted as encouraging competition at the lower levels, or should they take a strong and active and committed stand against this kind of practice.

DR. EAVES

I can't really speak on behalf of the other sports governing bodies, but I really think that maybe what you have to say in terms of their looking at competition might be true. I don't know if they are, here again I am speaking for them and I really shouldn't. As far as the CAHA is concerned I will direct my remarks towards them. One thing that Hockey Canada has done is acted as a catalyst, and we talk about Change Agent Research, Hockey Canada has actually been the catalyst for the CAHA in terms of having them look at themselves. Now, hopefully through some kind of government involvement and the continuance of Hockey Canada in some form, the CAHA will be in a position to continue to look at what we are doing and I really think in part that this was one of the reasons that Murray and I were hired, to provide some insight and some sensitivity from the tradition that has been there for fifty-seven years.

Just a general comment in terms of the other sports, you must realize that there is seemingly a nationalistic approach developing in terms of basketball and say track and field and swimming. In order for Canada to compete with other countries they feel that its very possible to get the kids started at a very young age, because in Russia they are starting their hockey players at four and five years old and they are starting their figure skaters at four and five and really by the time they are fourteen or fifteen they have reached their peak, and where do they go from there. So really maybe its follow-the-leader type of thing.

Question

Yes, except at some times we follow the wrong leader and end up with disastrous results, and if I may I would like to address a question to Dr. Loy. It comes back to comments made by the Mayor earlier regarding this tremendous drop-off at age fourteen plus, and I am wondering what it would take to stimulate some of our fellow academicians, particularly in the sociology of sports area or the social psychology of sports area to start researching the area of what kinds of activities and what kinds of organization. What type of environment would satisfy, would attract, would involve the youngsters at that age group? Now, while the Mayor has a real concern that we all share for the rise in juvenile delinquency, I have an additional concern that would enhance their development. So the question really is what would it take for some of our fellow academicians to start researching this area to present a theoretical base, to present some of the information that could act as a framework for the practitioners who could then take this talk with some of the youngsters and start developing the kinds of programs that would mean that youngsters fourteen to eighteen get back into some activity, either play or sport?

DR. LOY

I don't know if I can reply to that in any concrete way. For one thing my own bias is such that with my own research I view play as very intrinsic. I don't care to have someone tell me where my research should be directed, because it becomes an instrumental type. So, I don't know how many would like to devote themselves to those certain concerns. It's a slow process. So many times that we have to place too much faith and hope in terms of what research results are going to produce. For example, we have had fifty years of white rat research now. Thousands and thousands of studies, and just in the last half dozen years or so. Since so little has been done on sport if indeed we were to invest in untold amount of moneys and manpower to look at many of these things that we have raised here, I think that it may be a good idea. I am not sure that the results are going to be quick or effective. So that is one type of response.

I think so much of it is just a matter of power, who has the power to bring about change, and who wants to. How do you get access to that power, be it money or political control? Or how do you structure sport? I think it is a matter of social conflict type theories and I think that is the sorts of theories to use, and what is the most effective way to lead different types of minor results. That type of research would be more use than anything directed to sport per se. I think a lot of this is the normal part of the life span in terms of how we structured our roles. If you look when things begin to drop off, this is when kids get to the point that they have a lot of choices. So to teenage high school boy or girl sport is just one of many things. Once one becomes married all of a sudden all of these doors are closed. Once the first child arrives other sorts of doors are closed. That does not mean that they cannot be unlocked again.

External change is going to have more influence on sport than anything that is done within sport.

"ATHLETICS AND THE BIG DOLLAR"

Jim Finks
General Manager
Minnesota Vikings

Bruce Kidd
Columnist and Former
International Athlete

Bernie Parrish
Former N.F.L. Star and Author—
"They Call It a Game"

Ken Fathers (Chairman)
Assistant Sports Editor
"The Windsor Star"

Jim Finks
General Manager
Minnesota Vikings

Needless to say, the first forty-five minutes of this part of the Seminar has left me a little confused. I didn't realize that it was going to be as heavy as it has been, and I hope that I am capable of responding in some form because if you have ever seen a prototype of the system, you're looking at one now, and for that I don't apologize.

Ken did tell you that I did attend university on an athletic scholarship and had it not been for that scholarship I would not have had the opportunity to attend. Had it not been for my athletic ability I wouldn't have gotten the scholarship naturally, and from that point I did go into professional sports, playing my first year of football in 1949 and without exception I have been in professional football with the exception of one year ever since. I spent one year at the University of Notre Dame as an assistant football coach.

I am very shocked to hear some of the remarks and references made to pro sports. Believe me, it's not all bad! I said at the outset I was most interested in Bruce's remarks because some of them hit very close to home. I heard "American Go Home" when I won in Canada in 1957 and Canadians were talking primarily about the oil people at that time, and I suppose they still are. But, I do not apologize for my twenty-seven years in sports and certainly I don't apologize for the seven-and-a-half years I spent in the Canadian Football League.

My first exposure to professional sports was in 1949, when I played for the Pittsburgh Steelers. From that point until today I have been in the Sport World and I have seen tremendous changes. I want to start with 1949 and then bring it up until today. There were eleven teams playing in the National Football League in 1949. Each club had a roster of thirty-two players. The average attendance for games then would be in the neighbourhood of twenty-five thousand per game. Naturally, a couple of the cities such as New York and Chicago and Los Angeles would draw a little bit more than that. The Pittsburgh, Philadelphia and the Chicago Cardinals and teams like this were playing before about twenty-five thousand. Of the thirty-two players the average salary was in the neighbourhood of six thousand dollars. Period, full stop. No fringe benefits, no endorsements. It wasn't very commercial and it was a lot of fun. The ownership at that time was comprised of people like Mr. Art Rooney of the Pittsburgh Steelers who was not wealthy. He has more money today than he had in 1949, but I suggest that he didn't make it in football. Mr. George Hallis who was an athlete all his life was the owner-coach of the Chicago Bears and had a laundry on the side. Mr. Tim Mera was of all things a bookmaker and a very well-respected bookmaker in New York, I might add. One hundred people owned the Philadelphia Eagles, and not knowing what their P & L would be in those times because I didn't have privy to it. I venture to say that eighty percent of the clubs lost money every year. But these men, true sportsmen that they were, were looking for something after the collegiate careers to have some fun and stay involved and do a service for the players and the fans.

Well, in 1949, and I mention only the National Football League, players played about two or three years hoping to get some start in life and usually after the third year they were looking towards another profession. My, how things have changed.

From 1949 to the present as far as fans are concerned, if you're not averaging fifty thousand people per game, financially you are in trouble. Rather than having eleven teams with a roster of thirty-two you now have twenty-six teams with rosters of forty-seven. The average salary today has been speculated by the player union. We don't have those numbers but I can speak with some authority about the other twenty-five teams. I can tell you this, the average salaries with the Minnesota Vikings are in excess of thirty-five thousand dollars per year. In addition to that, each player costs the Vikings approximately seven thousand dollars a year per man in funding his life insurance, his hospitalization, his pension and other benefits. That's forty-seven men.

Ownership has changed also, I get a kick out of everybody putting such a value on franchises. If you can go out and buy a national football franchise today for five or six or seven million dollars buy it. It would be a pretty good investment. But paying the kind of money that they are paying now for franchises doesn't make sense. It doesn't make sense. And, I would also point out that the "Meras" and the "Hallises" and the "Rooneys" bought franchises for ten or fifteen or twenty thousand dollars, twenty or twenty-five years ago. I would like to have the money that they lost during that twenty or twenty-five year period. I wouldn't worry about working any more.

The point that I am making is that on the surface it appears and we are led to believe that every franchise owner (and I guess it's unlimited, according to Bernie Parrish) makes (as he said on his telephone conversation) many times over five hundred thousand dollars per year. That is totally inaccurate. It's one of the problems that we are having today. These statements are being kicked around by uninformed people as to the kind of money that is being made by ownership in the National Football. And, I hope that you would appreciate my position. I sound like management and I am management, but I have been on all three sides of the table. I have been a player of the National Football League, I have been a coach and I am general manager now with Minnesota for ten years and seven in Calgary. So, I think I have a pretty good feel of all sides. In '49 I described to you where we were then, the number of fans, the kind of fans that were available. Thirty-two times eleven teams. I brought you up to '73 showing this fantastic growth and really the growth didn't start in '49. It really started to take off in '60 and '61. So the phenomenal growth that you have seen in the National Football League has been limited primarily to the last ten or eleven years.

What's happened, why did this all of a sudden catch the imagination of the fans in North America? Well, I feel the basic reason why the National Football League has caught the imagination and has a love affair with the American public is because of the basic policies that have been established by the league to create one situation, and that is competitive equality. Without competitive equality you have nothing, and all the policies that the National Football League are operating under today in my view have created competitive equality. It's eliminated the very, very wealthy owner. Other areas of the policies that have been adopted by the National Football League was the sharing of gate receipts. Obviously Cleveland with an eighty thousand capacity stadium financially would be better than Minnesota with a forty-seven thousand capacity stadium. This has been taken into consideration and not just recently. This goes back years and years ago, whereby Minnesota plays in Cleveland and they get three percent of that gate. When Cleveland plays in Minnesota they get forty percent of our gate. So in the final analysis we are getting more money from Cleveland than they are getting from Minnesota. This in a way balances. More recently is the sharing of television revenue between the twenty-six clubs. If we did not have this what would the Green Bay Packers television revenue be worth? The city of Green Bay is a hundred and fifty thousand compared to New York, Los Angeles or Chicago. The owners could have taken a position, "Well this is my market and whatever I can generate will be mine and whatever you can generate you can keep." They decided that this is what they were looking for, this would not give us the balance that we need so they are now sharing gate receipts as well as T.V. But, more probably the revenue would be the basic philosophy of giving every club an equal opportunity to get talent, and without talent you're not going to have winning football clubs.

The player selection which was put into effect over thirty years ago, commonly referred to the "players draft" whereby the team finishes with the poorest record gets first choice at all the college players the following year. The waiver system allows the weaker clubs to get first opportunity to put a claim in for this person. This always gives the weaker club a chance.

The option compensation clause, more commonly referred to as the Rossell Clause. Mr. Parrish made reference to the fact that players are in bondage for life. I don't know if you are familiar with the option compensation clause or not, but basically what it concerns is a player when he signs a contract to play in '73 and that contract has also an option, the club's option to exercise for '74.

Now, if he plays in '73 and he is unable to get together financially with the club that he has assigned with, he can choose to play out his option. It takes no further action. He can play the '74 season on his option. At the end of the '74 season he is what we call a "free agent". Now that means that he is free to contact any one of the twenty-five clubs in this case to see if they are interested in his services. This has been done time and time again. Probably the most famous one and the one that you will identify with would be the Joe Cap option to play out with Minnesota. Joe decided he was more valuable than we had determined.

To make a long story short, Joe signed later that summer with the New England Patriots at a tremendous salary and the Vikings were compensated. Now on the surface the approach that some people are taking with this is very unfair because if a player plays out his option, the club that he is leaving has to be compensated any way so that kind of dilutes his market value. You can't prove to me a case where this is true. Joe decided that he wanted to play with New England and New England decided that they would pay him as much as he wanted. The Vikings were compensated and everything was O.K., but if you didn't have that option to compensation clause what kind of a dilemma would we have.

If you say a club such as the Los Angeles Rams decided that they have a great football club, the only thing that they need would be the front four of the Minnesota Vikings. I think they might be right. What would prevent the Los Angeles Rams from suggesting to the four Vikings to play out the options and we will offer you each two hundred thousand dollars a year. If they can afford to pay that is all well and good. But where does that leave the Minnesota Vikings who have developed these players over a long period of time? They have spent a lot of money, done an awful lot of coaching and suffered through many downers before these fellows developed. You see what would happen. The Vikings would be then forced to take some sort of action. You would have constant turnover of your personnel every year, and in the final analysis, the very very rich franchises would end up with all the good football players, and you would destroy the one thing that has made the National Football League what it is today. A competitive balance.

I am not suggesting that these rules are foolproof. We are ready for changes, there is no question about it. If there is a better way of handling the player situation than we are doing right now let's talk about it. I think there must be. I suggest that we have to be firm in every area that we are operating in right now, but until somebody comes along with a better idea where we won't lose that one thing that we must have where it won't throw the league out of balance. And, what happens when you throw the leagues and teams out of balance. You are going to see it in the WHA franchises that are going to fold. Only the very very rich and very very wealthy are going to be able to stay, and what an injustice that can be to some cities and I might add whether the building was built by municipal funds or whether it was built by private funds. Let's not lose sight of the fact that it is fine entertainment for the Canadian as well as the American. It adds something to society. I am not suggesting that everything should be professionalized.

I have four children, four boys and we live in a community that is very very pressured and oriented to hockey. One of my sons who is sixteen now played Bantam two or three years ago, they were fortunate enough to be the national champions. They would play upwards to seventy games a year, and when they weren't playing they were practicing and I have seen these young fellows get so tired and so much pressure on them that it affected them. I reject this, I don't accept it, there must be better ways. But, I am dealing primarily with the national football view today, which I am more comfortable talking about than I am in other areas. But, I would say this to you contrary to what you hear about the National Football League, about how unfair it is, how one sided it is. What a shafting the players are taking. I take exception to these kinds of comments because people who make these kind of statements have no foundation, and they have nothing to back it up.

We are really in a business and nobody is denying that. We're in the entertainment business and we have to be competitive with the theatre. We have to be competitive with hockey. We have to be competitive with baseball, racetracks. We are in the entertainment business and nobody is suggesting that we are in anything else. It just so happens that we are in a position of attracting the very best athlete in North America. If everything was as bad as people have led some people to believe, and if I were a young guy it would turn me off, I wouldn't want to be involved in the National Football League. Do you know what a monopoly is Bruce?

BRUCE KIDD

The National Football League is certainly a monopoly.

JIM FINKS

Well, obviously he doesn't know what it is. Because the National Football League has been under scrutiny by the Justice Department and probably closer than any other industry in the last five years. The Justice Department has never suggested that we are a monopoly. We just had a grand jury hearing in Cleveland that lasted over a year.

BRUCE KIDD

Well, I don't have a staff of Philadelphia lawyers. You know you don't have any opposition in the United States, and from a commercial point of view, each of your franchise members, I think, has a monopoly in its territory.

JIM FINKS

You think.

Well, a monopoly would indicate to me that nobody else can come in. They're blocked out. Now, Bruce you know that is not true, but we will get back to that later.

I think through dialogue, and I think through exchange of ideas and conversations we can get on the same basis.

I'll tell you how unique the National Football League is. They have done a good job for the players. I think that they have opened the eyes of some of the owners. I think that they have opened the eyes of the public. You know there are some things that should be done. We have some sound thinkers in the National Football League. The biggest percentage of our fellows are college graduates, which means nothing necessarily, but they are good solid people, and they are organized and they have done some great jobs. Their union negotiates on all economic matters and working conditions, with the exception of one, and that is their own individual salaries. Now that is pretty unique. Now Bernie works for the teamsters. You know it's a great union. But, when they negotiate for a group of employees they negotiate everything, hospitalization, pension, vacations, hourly wage, bonus, and everything else.

Well, the players association is so unique that on one hand they're bargaining collectively on all of these things, but each player retains the right to negotiate his own individual contract. I think that it is extremely fair. It is pretty expensive, but it is extremely fair.

Now, I mentioned the average salary of the Vikings give or take a thousand either way. I don't know what the average in the National Football League is. I know our players' payroll is probably one of the largest in the National Football League, and it should be. I also mentioned the other dollars that go into funding a player in excess of seven thousand dollars a year for pensions.

Let me tell you how important and how good the pension is. It came home to us in a very sad way this summer. One of our very good football players had a motorcycle accident the day before training camp started and he was a ten year veteran. He is totally and permanently disabled. In the pension that the National Football League have for the players it states that if a player, depending on the years, becomes totally and permanently disabled he would start receiving the full payments that he would normally receive at age of 65. He will get $850.00 a month for life. Plus the fact that all of his hospitalization and doctor bills will be taken care of. I think that is a wonderful thing.

So, these are the plusses of being in the National Football League. What an opportunity it is for these young athletes to get a running start on life. The biggest mistake the athlete makes today, and I can see it in hockey and football and baseball, is they are led to believe they can play a few years of professional sports and become a rich man. If you expect to become rich playing football in the National Football League go somewhere else, because it is not in the cards. A good start in life, a great opportunity, a lot of education, a lot of other benefits, but get rich? No never. Not the players, not the owners.

One other facet to consider, is the fan, and the responsibility of the sportsman to the fan. Competition has made this fan, and I think we have a tremendous responsibility beyond the competition in the field. I think that the National Football League is always aware of the fan. People were making reference to the amount of dollars charged now to see a ball game, and the seats are sold out, and nobody can buy a ticket unless your grandfather willed it to you. Well, that is the situation in a lot of cities, but it didn't happen overnight.

This started in Minnesota. When I first went to Minnesota in the fall of 1964 they were averaging around thirty-five thousand people at all their games and it didn't change in '65 and it didn't change in '66 and it got a little bit better in '67 and not much better in '68, but we started winning, and now we are experiencing capacity crowds. You can't buy a ticket any more for our ball games. I don't apologize for that. I don't think that is cause for all of a sudden to say let's telecast boys. I think Congress acted too quickly. Bernie Parrish said that as far as he has been able to determine lifting the blackout hasn't affected any clubs. I don't know what he calls affecting, Miami has had eighty thousand no shows in five home games. Eighty thousand no shows. And, believe me it is not the economics this time. Where I am afraid it is going to affect the club, is the crowd reaction and the effect that the crowd has on the teams. Our players, our coaching staff and everybody in our organization feel that the enthusiastic live sport that we get in Minnesota gives us a great advantage when we are playing at home. And, I am just afraid that if this T.V. policy that we are saddled with for this year through the '75 season stays in effect, stays in force, we are going to see more no shows; and this is going to affect the performer. Football was not made to be a theatre game. It is meant to be played before live, enthusiastic crowds, and believe me speaking as a player, an ex-player and a coach, without that kind of support you can see the game deteriorating.

Bruce Kidd
Columnist and former
International Athlete

The first issue considered is the dilemma of sport and/or athletics in Canada and the United States. The focal point of this Seminar is properly understood as an inevitable consequence of the private enterprise system. I will argue that the evils and what the faculty here defines as athletics can primarily be attributed to the institution of private property relations, not the human imperfections as the Mayor of Denver suggested yesterday, although these imperfections do play their part. As I find the terms commercial sport and non-commercial sport to be more meaningful than athletics or sport these will be the terms that I will use.

Secondly, I will argue that the colonization of Canadian sport by American sport has been aided immeasurably by the institution of commercial sport and that the process has been a harmful one.

And, thirdly, that seminars of this kind only serve to retard the development of the more humane, more democratic sporting culture in Canada, because they set out to treat the problems of sport in these two countries as being nearly identical. That proposition is as dubious as the recent awarding of the Nobel Peace Prize to Henry Kissinger and Le Duc Tho on the basis that they play equal roles in the Indo-Chinese war.

At the outset let me say that I am not interested in merely describing our present sports scene as many have done here, but I also want to change it. What I want to see created is a sporting culture that will provide opportunities for everyone, regardless of class, sex, or age; to learn how to enjoy their physical selves, through some form of physical education, recreation, and to develop their physical strength and skills to whatever levels they set out for themselves. I believe that this cannot happen if private enterprise continues to rule in sport.

Also, at the outset, let me make one crucial distinction, between commercial and professional sport. Professional sport is a practice of paying a salary to an athlete or a coach, or to a manager, and this is something that I think is eminently desirable. It seems to me that any society is enriched if gifted members, whether they be athletes or scientists or painters or musicians, have an opportunity to pursue their talents to the fullest, and because everybody has to eat you have to pay them in order to do that. But commercial sport is something different, commercial sport is sport for buying and selling.

Most professional sport has been commercialized in Canada and the United States, although not always in other places. One exception was the Winnipeg and Ottawa based national hockey team which the National Hockey League persuaded a compliant Hockey Canada to disband in the spring of the 1970's. Some amateur sport has been commercialized too. Indoor track and field is one example. It is only recently that attempts have been made to professionalize indoor track and field as well. Well, O.K. How does commercialization limit and distort opportunities for physical culture in Canada? In the first place, it militates against the achievement of excellence. Private enterprise means profit maximization, that in turn, means the maximization of revenues. So to sell as many seats as possible you lengthen the schedule, and to fatten the television contract you expand your league to the west coast. The result is conditions that make excellence all but impossible. Take the NHL for instance, more than a hundred games a year including exhibitions and play-offs. Almost one hundred thousand miles of travel in the air, jumping from time zone to time zone, without any chance for acclimatization. Little time to practice, almost a different bed every night. No wonder we get barely twenty minutes of hockey in every sixty minute game, and the league tries to cover up its mediocrity by debasing the skills of stick handling, shooting, skating, and passing and substituting instead of kneeing and holding, fighting and dumping the puck in. Now to be fair not every NHL owner is in favor of "watering down the whiskey," as Clarence Campbell once described it, but it is an inevitable dictate of the laws of capitalistic economics.

The second consequence of commercialization is re-education in the number of opportunities to watch and play the game. Another desiderata of profit maximization is monopoly. It permits the owner to charge as much as he wants for as many seats as he cares to sell. More often, there will be the high price monopolies of commercial sport. That's what the war between the WHA and the NHL is all about. The trouble is that inevitably it limits the number of teams per single community.

In the book that John and I wrote "The Death of Hockey," we documented how the NHL in its drive for monopoly pushed a number of good entertaining and professional and semi-professional community teams out of business in the 1930's and 1940's and the 1950's. Kraft is doing the same thing in the dairy industry today. Monopoly is bad for the players too, as Eagleson told us yesterday. But it doesn't have to be that way, if you eliminated the owners and you eliminated their profits to say Toronto, where on the average the dividends each year amount to twice the salary bill. You could have three teams playing one-third of the number of games, and much, much better hockey.

In Australia where that crazy game of Australian football is not commercialized there are thirty-two professional and semi-professional teams in the city of Melbourne alone. Each small community then has its own teams, something that we had in hockey long, long ago, we should have it again. That's why I attacked Eagleson and the NHL Players' Association yesterday. If they were really concerned about monopoly they would try to smash it, instead they have just joined as partners.

One more example, the commercial leagues need players who fit into its system, so it must supervise their training. And it does this in two ways.

First, by controlling the minor and amateur leagues, the way the NHL does, the CAHA by bribing it, and this has been frequently documented. The result is a sharp reduction in opportunities for players no longer potential professionals. The most insidious example of this is now ruling in the senior OHA, the Ontario Hockey League right here. The ruling limits each team to five players over the age of twenty-three, three years over the NHL universal draft, and the OHA still sees itself as a farm team for the NHL. That's why hockey, a game that should and could be played by both men and women until at least they are sixty, is only played by boys in this country.

And, the second method of apprenticeship is the manipulation of the mass media. In hockey the chief instrument of NHL socialization is Hockey Night in Canada, as we talked about this morning. One result is the identification by all sport fans, with the gladiatorial ethics of commercial sport; and the confusion between the ideals of sport and athletics as defined here, which prompted this Seminar.

It's Hockey Night in Canada where parents are encouraged to push their kids into commercialized hockey. These problems several people mentioned this morning. If the only sports legitimized by the media are male-oriented and played only by boys and a few professionals, then no one else is encouraged to take part.

Well there are many more examples of commercialization's harmful impact on sports. I have used the example of hockey, but the same points can be made elsewhere. Of course, other factors are active too. The role of parents is obviously true when one is discussing the problems of hockey, but as I just suggested the behavior of parents and other groups is heavily influenced by the media, the cheerleaders of commercial sport.

The second point that I would like to make is the Americanization of Canadian sport is largely a result of this commercialization. Those of us who live in this country are painfully aware of the extent of Americanization of sports and Physical Education: the text books, the professors' legitimization of U.S. competition, the pursuit of apprenticeship by both Canadian athletes and would-be academicians in American universities, and so on and so on.

Virtually every aspect of the sporting experience here is either determined or heavily influenced by the American experience. What I find most galling is the wholesale exploitation of our national game, hockey. Developed by thousands and thousands of Canadians, coaching, teaching, driving kids to the rinks, building arenas with their tax dollars, buying equipment and ice time, for the entertainment of American sports fans, and the profits of American businessmen. What other country would allow the highest form of its national sport to be primarily sold in another country? The dominance of the most influential Canadian sports by American business should not be surprising after all. If American businessmen did not invent the institution of commercial sport, they certainly perfected it. They had the capital, the know-how, and the markets, and because our sport has been commercialized too, it was vulnerable.

So, in the first big wave of expansion in the 1920's the American sports entrepreneurs swallowed up their Canadian counterparts all but Conn Smythe and the Canadian Arena Company in Montreal. By and large other Canadian businessmen stood idly by, if they did not actively encourage this process. I think of the years of eagerness to sell, of men like Lester Patrick who sold the entire western Canadian hockey league to Boston, New York, Pittsburg, Detroit and Chicago in 1926; men like Percy Thompson who owned the first place Hamilton Tiger team that became the New York Americans, when he sold it in 1925; I think this and the reluctance of the other Canadian businessmen to invest in commercial sport right down to the present day, can be explained by the mercantile character of the majority of Canadian businessmen. That propensity for portfolio investment that led them away from actual entrepreneurship. This characteristic is best described by Professor Tom Naylor of McGill University in his article "In Class and The National Question in Canada," edited by Garry Tepple. I mentioned Naylor because his thesis about the economic values and behaviors of Canadian businessmen seems to be very close to what I understand are Professor Alan Metcalf's finding of the sporting values and behavior of these very people. It helps to explain why the takeover was so sudden and so without struggle. I think the analysis of Naylor, Metcalfe, and others also helps explain why public programs of sport, physical education and recreation in Canada have been so undernourished.

The predominantly mercantile Canadian elite has always seen itself to be a junior partner to empire and, as a result, it relied on the metropolitan country, first Britain and now the United States, to provide the technological and ideological leadership. And, so, it is miserly investments in education documented by John Porter and others, particularly in higher education. We also suffer from the fact that these people, the Canadian elite, developed its first major sporting idea in institutions on the Victorian model, a model categorically opposed to the support of mass participation in sport, other than for military training, when a world war was in process. So when public education was neglected, public physical education was even more neglected. I think that we had a really good example of this yesterday when Roger Rousseau talked about the fact that no government in this country is prepared to invest in the Olympics. No government in this country is prepared to sell the idea that the Olympics would be good for this country and put money into it. And, so what Rousseau and COJO are having to do is finance the games by resorting to gambling, monetary speculation and a close association with commercial sports. All these kinds of things which the Olympic movement supposedly is against, and that is because the ruling allegiance in this country has always been very very reluctant to invest public money in the development of opportunities for sports and play.

I believe the Americanization of sport is extremely harmful to us for it reinforces our cultural colonization. Imagine, little league hockey players all over this country emblazon on their shirts names like the Minnesota North Stars, or the Los Angeles Kings, or the Chicago Black Hawks, or the Atlanta Flames; and we have all seen this, where generations of high school athletes are being encouraged to accept U.S. athletic scholarships.

Have you ever sat down and tried to figure out what it does to their head. You know what it does, it tells them that what happens in this country really doesn't amount to very much. The big apple and where it is at, where things really count, is in the United States. And, of course, all this is reinforced by the fact that it is the leaders of our country that are pushing them to this other country, who won't provide them opportunities so that they could stay here.

Analogous to this is John Hershey's child buyer in the novel where the little kid is so disgusted by how the computer company can buy all his friends and his parents and everybody else that he sells himself, because he doesn't want to be around any longer. And, I think all of us know of Canadian athletes who wanted to stay in the country but eventually accepted a U.S. scholarship or a job in the United States because there wasn't any opportunity up here. What it does is reinforces our colonization in a very very strong way.

No wonder Canadians seem so apathetic and powerless. No wonder survival is that dominant theme in Canadian literature as Margaret Atwood has shown. No wonder the male heroes of Canadian films, as argued by Bob Fathergill, are invariable cowards, and bullies and clowns. The most serious consequence of this is that it prevents us coming to terms ourselves with our own experience. Whenever we have a problem, we import somebody else's solution; and the fact that hockey, our national game, is played out in another country over and over again and we imitate that, reinforces this. There is an even more harmful consequence I think of the Americanization of Canadian sport.

Sport, as I think everyone agrees, can be a powerful vehicle for ideology. The Americanization of Canadian sport reinforces the myth of the "American dream" in Canada and the belief in the private enterprise system. Free trade and supposedly free flow of ideas. All of which acclimatize Canadians to the take over of every aspect of our society by American business, our oil, our gas, our minerals, our television entertainment, our universities, our publishers, even our funeral parlors.

A friend of mine, Gregg Colonels, a London artist, has a slogan, "Close the 49th parallel, increase the flow of information and ideas and exchanges with people of everywhere else," says Gregg, "but close the 49th parallel." It's wildly impractical but it would be a very good idea.

I think that my third point should be clear by now. Canada and the United States do not face similar problems in sports or in any other field. But, one of our chief problems is U.S. domination so seminars like this one only confuse the issue, of course, they benefit the American multinational corporation like the National Hockey League, which takes all our best young hockey players produced by thousands of people and sells it for its own profit in the United States.

For the Canadians who are struggling for self-direction and independence I don't have very many answers. It's going to be a very long hard struggle. The media is not controlled by us, capitalism in North America is exceedingly strong and while it's going through some horrendous problems right now it is certain to survive them. We are just going to have to dig in and do as much as we can. It seems to me that there are two levels where we can operate. The first is to press governments that are sympathetic to do a number of things. First, provide more money for coaching, more money for facilities, especially more money so that we can train people to teach Physical Education in the schools. How many trained people are there in the primary schools in this country to teach Physical Education? No wonder so many people are so intimidated by it. We have got to end the private problem.

We have got to put pressure on governments to do that. We've got to put pressure on government to put some controls over the media. You know the CBC is supposedly publicly owned; and we should be able to use the CBC to regain control of Hockey Night in Canada, that institution that provides so much propaganda for the NHL. It seems to me that we are not powerless in the face of that kind of domination. We ought to be able to use that institution to teach the values that are important to us, and to revolutionize and change the way the young kids learn sport in this country; and we should put pressure on friendly governments to take over where possible, big sport.

I have been arguing with a former colleague of mine in B.C.; what we should have done a long time ago is take over the Vancouver Canucks, and without compensation too; and there is a lot that he could do with that. He could lower the price of tickets and so the profits, that Al Eagleson pointed out are quite incredible; he could lower the price of tickets. He could break up the monopoly of season tickets that exists in Vancouver, so a lot more people could watch the game. He could do a great deal to change the character of hockey in that town. He could use his clout with the broadcasting system. As you know the arena from which the broadcasts eminate have an incredible amount of control of what goes into broadcasting. He could use all of these things. If we have friends like that, we have got to put pressure on them. You know governments don't listen very well to good ideas, and good ideas don't of themselves get implemented. Even if this is very small, some of those changes can mushroom into something bigger.

There are a lot of exciting things that are happening at the very minor level of organized sport in this country. Parents and teachers are saying "Hey, wait a minute the emperor has no clothes." The example of the National Hockey League and other commercial sports is not an example that we want to follow any more, and they are experimenting with changes. There is an experiment that Edmonton began last year in their children's program, which had the same kinds of results. I think it was even a bit more encouraging, and there are similar experiments all over.

We have got to see that it is our sport, and we ought to be controlling it. We have got to fight to get more women involved in sports. I can give you a long list of things that we ought to be doing. There is a lot that we can do and let's get out and do it.

Bernie Parrish

Former N.F.L. Star and Author
"They Call It a Game"

I am looking at professional sports from a little different standpoint than I have over the past years as I was growing up in them. Most people look at sports, including professional sports, from the aspect of either just fun and games or sportsmanship's high display of morality, integrity. It is also important to many people because of the influence it has on youth.

As a player representative of the Cleveland Browns, I began to be concerned about the economic aspect of the game, and now as a businessman I look at it even more so from the economic standpoint.

The Brookings Institution made a very interesting and accurate analysis of professional football in economics and they were very much concerned with the aspect of public financing of the stadiums and their resulting operational losses which were really astounding. Some eight hundred million tax dollars (public financing) has been poured in plush new stadiums in recent years and the plusher and the newer of these stadiums, the more operational losses are incurred. The newer more plush ones average about five hundred thousand dollars a year loss. From the cities' standpoint or the municipalities' that operate them and this, of course, is brought about from the strength of the franchise owners negotiating position with the municipalities. The franchise owner is part of a monopoly, and all that he has to do is move from Milwaukee to Atlanta (and more recently other moves) to get a better deal on a stadium. So the city is in a very poor negotiating position and this, therefore, makes the public financing of public stadium really a very poor investment. Then, that publicly financed stadium turns out to be a money factory for a private individual who is the franchise owner. Now, he certainly doesn't lose a half a million dollars a year. He makes many times that in net profits each year. Even the privately financed stadiums require public financed parking lots and access streets.

The problem, as I see it, is forty years down the pike somebody is going to have to pay the bill; and it sure is not going to be the franchise owners, and it is not really going to be the number of fans who own season tickets and who frequent the stadiums. It is going to be paid by the public at large, by the municipality which is funded by the taxpayers at large.

The public really has a great stake in professional football and all sports from the stadium financing standpoint. But, the greatest economic impact on the public really is the impact from the twenty billion dollars of tax free money that is generated from the coffers of organized crime from illegal bookmaking each year. There have been estimates on it from the Department of Justice in the United States from seven billion (that is not million, that's with a "B") to fifty billion dollars a year generated for the coffers of organized crime through illegal bookmaking and gambling on professional team sports as well as horse-racing. The thing that concerns me a great deal is that there is a syndromical triangle between professional sports, the news media and the national bookmaking syndicate which, of course, is controlled by organized crime and it seems to go unrecognized. The way it works is a bet makes the game more interesting for the fans. So, the newspaper, the media, supplies the fan bettor with his essential betting information. The point spread information about the team, etc. The normal information is not what concerns me but the item of information that really facilitates the betting is this publicizing the point spread which is done on a daily basis.

And, an interesting point is that Jimmy the Greek Snyder is now recognized as one of professional football's celebrities. He goes to professional football banquets around the country to make speeches. His name is probably mentioned more often on the sport pages than any other sports star whether it is Johnny Unitis or Joe Namath (or whoever). This is an interesting comment on how betting and illegal bookmaking have grown in recent years. The bettor's interest makes him a season ticket customer, a newspaper buyer, and a patron of the local bookie, who must pay off organized crime for their assistance in laying off his partisan fans over balanced bets which are on his books.

For instance, if New York is playing L.A., particularly on television, this stimulates a great deal of betting with the New York bookmakers because of the point spread balancing, whether New York has a good team or a bad team. The point spread makes it interesting for the partisan fan to back his own team because the point spread sort of equalizes things. So, the New York bookmaker is going to have a great number of bets on his books from the New

York fans, and the Los Angeles bookmakers will have the same thing on their teams.

So, somehow if one team wins, and bets, the point spread wins, the bookmakers in that particular city are going to take a terrible beating. So, somehow they have to protect themselves and organized crime provides the service. They provide the layout system by which the New York bookmakers lay off their bets or balance their books against Los Angeles bookmakers and for this they charge for services. The local bookmaker may seem to be a very fun-loving and fun sort of guy and a great guy to get along with. He cannot stay in business without patronizing the organized crime who really controls the layout system. Betting on professional sports and this, the layout system, is where organized crime derives the majority of their cash flow income. The betting on professional sport has become the prohibition era activity of today. In fact, the old bootleggers are the ones who really started and today control the layout system.

Before the Associated Press and the UPI started carrying the point spreads the Continental Press Wire Service which was based in Chicago and spread throughout the entire country, but operated extensively in the mid-west, was the principal distributor of the point spreads and the betting odds. And, for this bookmakers would pay the Continental Press Wire Services a weekly fee. In 1953 Senator Estes Keifauver called it public enemy number one. The owner and president of the Continental Press Wire Service in 1953 was Mickey McBride, who also happened to be the founder of my old alma mater the Cleveland Browns Professional Football Club; and he owned the club at the time, which, to me is somewhat of a comment on where professional football stands on the betting issue. And, I realize that 1953 was a long time ago, but I don't think things have changed that much.

What's the solution to this illegal bookmaking generating so much money and having such an economic impact on the country, which really dwarfs any economic impact which professional owners derived through their selling tickets or their television income?

The NFL today, I don't believe, nor does any other professional sport live up to the responsibility they have in facing this problem. They really deny that the problem exists. They want to minimize the extent of gambling that their fans do on their particular sports. That really is their policy, they simply have taken the position of professing the purity of their particular sport and claim that their particular brand of monopolistic corporate regulation is the only way to protect the integrity of the game. I really don't believe that. I believe that public interest must be protected by public servants who are answerable to the taxpayers ultimately. I realize that government regulation is not the answer to everything, and there are tremendous problems that go with that, as we see by Watergate and many other scandals. But, is it a better alternative than the present situation? I think it is. I think that in government regulation there is going to have to be a federal agency set up to govern professional sports not only from the monopolistic problems which caused the players great distress. Particularly in professional football where they are bound to one team for the life of their career, which becomes involved when going into the playing out of options and so forth which really is only the forcing of the trade. As long as the team has the tie to that player in some way (the employer that he is working for must give up something for him) he is tied to that team for life, no matter whether you label him as an agent after he does a certain amount of time for a team or not.

But, aside from those monopolistic problems (which are being dealt with to a minor extent by the NFL players' association, which is their union), the other problems which face professional sports (and really ultimately lead, and I think directly concerns the American public) is the protection of sports from this the illegal bookmaking operations. This comes far too close to the teams themselves than the general public may realize. And, it is policed really on a form of self-servicing standpoint rather than the protection of the public in general. Scandal is covered up rather than exposed and this really has been the general policy of most professional sports since the days of the Black Sox's scandal. But, the answer really in my mind lies in the legalization of gambling. Although I am no bettor and don't intend to become one, I believe that the legalization of gambling on a national basis is the only answer. I don't think that it should be done on a state-wide basis because as long as you can cross a line and make the illegal bet there is going to be advantages there. But, even legalized gambling is not going to put organized crime out of business. But, maybe it will take away half of that income. If we could just make a dint in the twenty billion and recruit maybe ten billion of it for the tax coffers and they tax that money, then that has got to be a benefit for the entire country.

The mood of government is changing. In talking with senators on the judiciary sub-committee on mergers which ruled on the conditional merger of the American Basketball Association and the NBA (which really nullifies the owners' interest in a merger by taking away their option clause or their reserve clause, and gives up the binding of a player to a team for life) if the owners had accepted, it would have nullified any advantage they would have gained through a merger. This was the first piece of legislation that has ever gone against the lobbying of professional franchise owners. Everything else has gone their way up to the ABA-NBA basketball merger, which the players' associations have combined together and blocked effectively.

Recently the blackout has been lifted by Congress which has caused a great deal of crying from the owners position but from the standpoint of the fans is really in their best interest; and if you really check the records, you will see that the decrease in attendance has not been that great. There has always been a certain number of no shows no matter what the event is, even to the selling of the airline tickets. I wish there had been a couple of no shows this morning, but at any rate, the no shows that the NFL is crying about right now is really not a lot more than they experienced in normal operation. I think that studies are going to show that.

The important thing is that the mood of government is changing, I hope that the mood of the public is changing and I hope that they realize that government regulation is the answer to many of the problems in professional sports, as more and more states and legislatures become concerned with the issues of illegal gambling and legalizing gambling.

I hope that the people who are listening to day are a little more aware of the problems, I hope that I have swayed them a little toward being sympathetic towards legalization of gambling and I hope that they will vote that way when they are faced with the issue.

Within the next few years I believe every citizen in the United States, and probably in Canada, will be faced with voting for or against the legalization of gambling. It is extremely important, and I think, it is probably the primary impact of professional sports in this country today.

Discussion Period

Question

Maybe if you lowered your prices for your games you would fill the stadium and then in the process, raise your rights for T.V. You would have a full stadium, and everyone would be happy.

JIM FINKS

Well, we have full stadiums.

Question

Well, tell that to Miami.

JIM FINKS

Well, they have full stadiums.

Question

Well, didn't you just say that they had eighty thousand no shows?

JIM FINKS

Yes, right. I don't think no shows relate to the amount of tickets sold. There is no relationship. No show means that now you see it on television I won't use my ticket. I will stay at home.

Question

O.K. How much does it cost for a ticket?

JIM FINKS

It varies. In Minnesota our top ticket is $7.00, which is a real bargain I might add.

Question

How about Miami. What is the lowest?

JIM FINKS

I would imagine $5.00. I don't see what you are driving at.

Question

Well, I am talking about the guy that just can't afford it.

JIM FINKS

Can't afford what? Economically it doesn't mean anything to us. But, we want to get the enthusiastic live crowd there. We don't want to be playing to that red light and half-full stadiums.

Question

Well, what I am trying to get at is the enthusiastic fan who can't afford to buy it, because these big corporations have bought all these sixteen thousand tickets; and this week we can only give away eight thousand so the other eight thousand are going to sit and no one is going to go to the game?

BRUCE KIDD

There are two aspects to the ticket question. One is the pricing and, of course, that is related to the ownership and profit expectations of the owners. And, the other is who gets to buy a ticket. Hockey Canada did something last year which I think ought to be followed everywhere. What they did is they put a single price for every seat in the house during the four Canadian games during the Canada/Russia series; and they allowed tickets to be drawn by lot, so that everybody in the community had an equal opportunity. It seems to me that is a much fairer way of allocating the seats than to allow someone to will a season ticket for generation after generation. I think that would be a much fairer way of getting people to see the games. Jim, it's more exciting to be there in person than it is to watch it on the tube.

Question

You presented a very strange paradox. You presented the beautiful image of your playing football as a child and in college. What a wonderful thing it was. Then you presented the image of your son, and I think that is the dilemma that we are worried about. I would like you to try and explain the paradox.

JIM FINKS

Well, it would simply be how times have changed. The community that I lived in and I grew up in certainly didn't approach the sport then the way that it is being approached now; and I think that I tried to say that I could identify and empathize with what Bruce was trying to say, about the pressures at certain levels.

Question

I am a Windsor boy (Canadian), and I would like to speak in defense of Jim Finks and some of my fellow colleagues. I happen to have the opportunity of playing Junior hockey here and participating in sports locally, and again an opportunity was presented to me which wasn't presented in Canada to go over to the States. I'm very grateful for having this opportunity and I am thankful and without it I don't think that I would be where I am today. It is a good thing to get a group of people togther like this to "knock heads" and talk about ideas. We are all basically interested in children and athletics and, pardon my expression, "we're making monsters out of this thing."

There is nothing wrong with competition. I have been away from hockey for a long time; and three years ago I got involved in coaching a hockey house-league, which I am very happy with. And, I have taught my kids to win in the proper light that they should win with humility. And, I saw a perfect example of this last night listening to Jesse Owens, and I think that this is true of all great athletes. There is a tremendous humility in these people. Even though they become professionals they still retain that. And, I was talking to one chap yesterday who played pro ball over here and he said "You know, it isn't the money aspect all the time; and we can't put a dollar sign on it all the time; and there is a certain amount of pride that the human individual has." Even in professional sports which I haven't played or propose to know that much about. I'm trying to refer to amateurism. Again there is nothing wrong with competition because you have to teach your kids to compete, and you can teach them this through sports whether it be hockey, football or baseball. I think that it is the attitude that we as parents, coaches, or whatnot teach these children to go out into the world and to grasp it in that light that somebody has got to win and somebody has to lose. And, you win with humility and you lose with dignity. I think that if we all learned this and went away with it, maybe we would be better citizens for it.

BRUCE KIDD

Let me restate my comment on athletic scholarship. I think the athletic scholarship possibility or opportunity to the United States was personally a good thing. I think the Canadian athlete faces a terrible dilemma, because there are very few opportunities in his own country, and you know there are these opportunities that are put forward in another country. I tried to make that point because I want to illustrate that the Canadian business class, the ruling league, in this country has rarely if ever provided real opportunities for people to develop themselves in various sports or any of the other cultural areas, thereby forcing people like yourself, if they wanted to develop themselves further in that activity, to leave and go to the United States.

Question

I would like to address my comments to Mr. Finks. He is reputed to be one of the most astute and possibly one of the most humane NFL general managers; but, I detected a little bit of inconsistency in some of his arguments. He stated that the NFL owners were very far-sighted in seeking competitive equality. One of the methods that they use is T.V. sharing and gate sharing, etc.; and, on the other hand, he turned around and said that they need the option compensation in order to protect the owners from themselves. In other words, on the one hand they are wise; but, on the other hand, they would be unscrupulous, they would buy up all the available talent and destroy the league. Do you see a contradiction there?

JIM FINKS

No. It is an excellent point, and exactly what we need is something to protect ourselves from our own greed. Excellent point. Even though this is a league, an association of twenty-six people who have gotten together to form this league, unless we do have these kind of rules that very thing would happen, and if you call it a contradiction, why it is a fact; it would happen!

Question

I can't see why one owner or a few owners would go out and would attempt to detroy this competitive equality that the whole league is seeking.

JIM FINKS

You can't imagine the tremendous desire to win in the National Football League by all clubs, if you identify with that.

Question

Another thing you mentioned is your concern for the welfare of your ball players; and I know that you have a lot of fringe benefits; but, on the one hand, all of the new stadiums, pretty well, have astro turf; and the players association has come out against playing on it. Yet, owners seem to be blind to this. They continue to make new stadiums with astro turf.

JIM FINKS

The owners aren't blind to it. There are studies now being done, so I suggest that it is a little too early to be conclusive one way or the other. Frankly, I don't like to see the game on synthetic. This is done out of necessity rather than choice. As a football man I would rather see it played on regular turf.

But, getting back into the economics of building the stadiums, to justify this you must in many cases have multiple use for the stadiums, baseball, football, rodeos, track and field and what else. And, the most practical way to do this is to have a synthetic. But, I still say contrary to what the players' association stand is, it is not conclusive whether it causes more injuries or less injuries. Until those studies are made, and they are in the process of making them right now, our position is, "let's just stay status quo." You can recall five years ago when everybody was advocating, "Install it because it will decrease the amount of injuries."

Question

But, you are opting again for economic necessity and not considering the welfare of the players.

JIM FINKS

Now, that is not true, and you know that is not true. I said the studies were not conclusive. Obviously, for self reasons we are interested in the health of our football players. I think that I can stand on that statement.

Question

You state that what would prevent any owner from going to any other team; and your example, you gave, was taking your front four.

JIM FINKS

I guess I should say in summary, it's very apparent the National Football League is not for everyone; but those who choose to go that way, and approach it in the proper way, won't ever regret having been a member or participant in the National Football League.

BRUCE KIDD

Well, I think that it is fair to say that the NFL is the most progressive commercial sports institution in North America. I think that goes without saying. It's not all bad for many of the players and it's certainly not bad for the owners. But, I think we have to ask whether that institution and other institutions like it, are good for society as a whole; and what I have tried to put forward today is the argument that it is not good for society as a whole . . . that it is very harmful. Jim Finks said he took exception to those comments. Well, as its representative, we wouldn't expect him to do otherwise.

"THE FUTURE: AND THE INFLUENCE OF THE MEDIA"

Douglas M. Fisher
Columnist
Member, Federal Government's
Task Force on Sports

Pearl Berlin
Research Professor
School of Physical Education
University of North Carolina

Jack Dulmage
Sports Editor
"The Windsor Star"

James H. Duthie (Chairman)
Faculty of Physical & Health Education
University of Windsor

Douglas M. Fisher
Columnist
Member, Federal Government's
Task Force on Sports

I interpret the subject as double-barrelled: that its chief stress is towards the future of sport, that secondarily, it should relate this to the media (i.e., press, radio, television, film) to that future.

In order to make this broad subject manageable let me fix largely on Canadian sport, rather than world or North American sport; further my emphasis will be on participation and its trends, rather than on spectators and "fandom".

Despite some recent and current engagement in sports organization my viewpoint is largely that of a student of sports history in Canada.

First, let me give short shrift to the media as having much of a role in the future of sport. Its role has been and will be largely peripheral or only mildly influential on the course of Canadian sport; that is, the elements of the media may be mirror—diary—gossip—promoter—and conduit of sporting matters; they are not catalystic or critical, interpretive or persuasive, in any moralistic or idealistic sense.

Sporting periodicals and journals first appeared in Canada about 100 years ago. In the period immediately preceding their emergence—i.e., 1835-1970—so-called "sporting" items began to appear in the daily and weekly press of British North America, many of them culled from British and U.S. sporting journals such as *Sporting Life,* the *Spirit of the Times,* etc. Local items, relating first to curling and cricket, then to horse-racing, snowshoeing, rowing and lacrosse began to appear in the 1830's and by Confederation most of the dailies had a column or so of "sporting items" on most days and by the early '70s many of them had what was called a "sporting editor". Also, by that time the telegraph companies were sending out results of major and regular sports events and by the Centennial time in Philadelphia and Ned Hanlan's great rowing victory there, these wire accounts were long, well-written, sent and received and put in print with speed, and more and more from the paper's "own correspondent" or a "special correspondent".

By 1875, in Canada, judging from the daily press, the pattern which is familiar to us today was pretty well set:

1. Editors knew that sports information was of interest to its readers; that they appreciated the latest results and gossip; that their material should support the local teams and athletes against teams and athletes from other places; that exploits in international competition by Canadians had an immense appeal and there could rarely be an excess in chauvinism, particularly when the Canadians were doing well or were competitive.

2. The first local, regional and national sporting heroes had been found and honoured.

3. The role of prominent people in the local and national community in sport as patrons and leaders and administrators was well-established and recognized in the media of the time.

4. The basic structure of Canadian sport and the theme of national competition and national championships, including age, class, was jelling very quickly on the model of lacrosse and snow-shoeing (i.e., associations embracing several communities were tending towards federations). In other words our sporting organization and administration was apeing the political organization of Canada and it had the same zest for constitutions, by-laws, inter-city and inter-provincial competition.

5. The minor role of sport in the educational system of the provinces had been set, as had the voluntary and rather exclusive (more and more into the '90s) activity in sports in the colleges.

6. The issue of professionalism versus amateurism had emerged by 1875 in snowshoeing, lacrosse, and rowing and its contentiousness (e.g. I.O.C.) has been going ever since, as one sees in the printed record or recalls from radio and TV coverage.

7. Gambling was widely-recognized, catered to by the media at the same time it was inveighed against . . . with horses, boxers, wrestlers, rowers, lacrosse men, etc.

8. A concern for facilities, equipment, training, coaching, competent referees and judges, fair admission prices, all can be found in the sporting press coverage in Canada by 1875 and by ten years later all these matters were reported on in detail, including rules of competition and challenges, the responsibility of communities and governments for facilities and communications.

9. By 1885 the entrepreneurs of sport—i.e., the Smythes, Eaglesons, Davidsons, Ballards—were at work; they were developing the associations between transport firms (boats and railways and telegraph companies) and sport; so were the links with sport as sponsors of ethnic groups, distilleries, breweries and hotel keepers.

10. A national, continental and international interest in sport was recognized by and reported in the media of the time; and by 1885 international competition, including trips to Europe, the U.S., even to the Antipodes, was part of the weft and warp of Canadian sports journalism.

11. The inter-play, even the interchangeability, between the reporter of sport as participant, as referee, as promoter, as entrepreneur, as talent-scout, in sport was all in place by 1885, along with clubs and associations with real estate, clubhouses, courses, fields, stands, etc.

12. The worth of sport, the great athlete, the attractive sporting event from a promotional and Chamber of Commerce attitude was also familiar and largely recognized in Canada by 1885. Indeed, we even had by then students who would go to American universities because of the opportunities offered there for sports participation.

What all this means, in the context of our subject, is that there's nothing new under the sun. Serious and highly moral men in Montreal in the early '80s decried the city's obsession with sport, and while the editorial page writers tended to agree, the sporting columns grew and grew in length and range of subject matter, almost steadily from 1870 to 1890. And by that last date, the pattern of professional sport organization and management had been well set, including something first cousin to the reserve clause.

Thus I argue that the role of the media in the future, as it is in the present, and as it was fixed long, long ago, is as mirror and reporter and conduit, not vital or crucial to the future of sport.

It is my judgement that in the century of substantial sporting activity we have had in Canada there has always been a substantial number of the society as a whole who take part in sport of an organized or relatively organized kind and an even larger number who could be described as fans or spectators. I think attendance figures at sporting events, small towns and big cities, bear this out, so does the relative space given sport in the media through that period. Indeed, since the 1900-1910 period, a golden age in Canadian sport interest and participation, the sporting side of all popular journalism has accentuated sport. Even the emergence of the sports columnists and the radio actuality in the '20s and TV in the '50s has had remarkably little effect on the content and the ethos of sport in the media. Therefore, I can't see any reason why the media should become critical or powerful in affecting the future of sport in Canada . . . certainly not as a vehicle for reform or change.

On this last point, another generalization: men and women who participate in sport as players, leaders, coaches and administrators are by and large conservative in their attitudes towards change. That is, traditions hang heavy, yet this is not Burkean traditionalism with a cherishing of the past. Rather, it is an obsession with the here and now, this year's play, league and team and championship. There are few, very few long term planners in organized sport and even fewer who examine the past as a lesson on how the future should be moulded. Thus, neither within sport nor within the coverage of sport in the media is there the evidence from the past that there will be major changes in the pattern of activity. Trends, evolutions, relative rise and relative fall or eclipse in various activity, these are always underway, usually almost glacially, but not radical change and re-orientation.

Therefore, if one is predicting one needs to note the few obvious but slow trends and judge whether they will stop or slow down or become one. For example, in the '20s we had what might be called an upsurge in sporting activity by women that seemed to be side-tracked by World War II and which is now slowly reasserting itself. I think it will creep on.

Another example is the involvement by the federal and provincial governments in sport. I'll spare the details but obviously such support is coming on rather steadily but in an evolutionary fashion, as is the development of the full-time administrator in national and provincial sporting fields. In relation to this last trend, we are certain to have tussles for a decade or two between the paid, full-time administrator and technical expert and the volunteer, elected leader of sports organizations and groups.

What is also clear is that the diversity of sporting opportunity, always rather large in Canada, since the 1880's, will continue to grow as the annual calendar and the years fill in with competition and events. Further, the "carry over" and "carry on" sports are going to increase and broaden, particularly those which have a "nature" component such as skiing, especially cross-country skiing, equestrianism, sailing, canoeing. The trend towards stressing fitness is almost certain to continue upwards for some years and I think there will be more and more recognition that the best means to attain this is through organized and competitive sport, rather than through dutiful exercise programs and specialized diets.

In summary, in the sporting future I see no radical changes for sport or for society, and most of what we have in place now will be there, more or less, in the early 2,000's as it was in the 1880's and 1890's.

Pearl Berlin
Research Professor
School of Physical Education
University of North Carolina

There are two specific perspectives in which I shall consider the general theme of the Seminar, "Sport or Athletics: A North American Dilemma," and the more particular focus of this session, "The Future: And the Influence of the Media." In discussing sport and athletics, my remarks concern girls' and women's involvement only. Time does not permit a full explication of the rationale for such an emphasis. But you are all aware of (1) the effects of the idea of "equal rights" on girls and women's physical activity interests and participation, (2) the enormous growth of female competitive sport programs, (3) the formulation — within women's movement organizations — of special groups concerned with sport, and (4) the serious study of women and sport that is taking place on many college campuses both in conjunction with women's studies programs and with the emergence of sport as a bonafide field of inquiry . . . To add a personal note, I would want you to know that as a woman whose life has been significantly influenced by sport and athletics, I am weary of the neglect and ignorance that has been associated with female participation in competitive physical activity.

The specific strategy for discussing the media borrows heavily from some of the ideas undergirding perceptual theory. Perceiving is, after all, fundamental to all behavior. By recognizing, selecting, organizing, integrating and interpreting data about our environment and ourselves as creatures within that environment, we come to know and to understand a myriad of things about our world. We learn. We perform skills. We relate to other human beings.

It was the noted Duke University Professor of History, Anne Firor Scott, who inspired me to approach the topic this way. Recently, I heard Dr. Scott (1973) talk about "the invisible woman" in history. Using one illustration after another from historical records, she set forth substantial evidence that most contemporary women are shaped by a history they do not know about!

My intent is to first share with you some information about female sport involvement. The facts and figures allow the inference to be made that *what we do not know* (and have not yet sought to find out) is, perhaps, far more than what we do know about women and sport. Furthermore, the data suggest that at this critical time of development of women's activity programs, our perceptions about participants, certain sport experiences, effects and other fundamental issues are likely to be based more on myths than on realities. In that regard, some comments will be made about human perceptual processes with special reference to the role of anticipation. Finally, a few brief remarks about the media as "perceptual double-agents" capable of influencing girls and women's sports will be offered.

Selected Facts About Women's Sport Involvement

According to Howell and Howell (1969), a factor that distinguished the period of time from Confederation to 1900 insofar as the study of sports and games in Canadian life is concerned is "greater acceptance of women in various fields of physical endeavour" (p. 67). The authors point out that tennis was considered to be "proper," swimming was encouraged, bicycling was pursued in spite of its consideration as unladylike and hockey teams were organized. They also report the following paragraph in the *Prescott Telegraph* the dateline of which is cited as October 31, 1879.

Football
Ottawa Young Ladies to the Front

There are six young ladies in the city of Ottawa, at present all unknown to fame, who are desirous of acquiring a reputation as athletes, and one of them has written us to say that they are willing to challenge any six young ladies in this town to a game of football, for a silver cup. We give their request publicity, but do not think there are any young ladies in Prescott who are ambitious to become champion football kickers (Howell and Howell, 1969, p. 68).

Prior to that time, in 1874, women in Canada ". . . were accepted as competitors in rifle matches" (Howell and Howell, 1969, p. 101). It was at the turn of the century that "women began to make their mark in curling, baseball, rowing, canoeing, basketball, swimming, track and field, skiing, sailing and even ice-hockey" (Howell and Howell, 1969, p. 146).

These historians point out that a changing role of women in athletics was noticeable, in particular, in the 1920's when "the Edmonton Grads basketball team competed successfully in Europe in 1926 and a Canadian girl, Rosa Grosse, set a new world record of 11.2 for the 100 yard dash" (Howell and Howell, 1969, p. 155).

According to Gerber's (1973) discussion of the historical antecedents of the present day sport scene in the United States, sport for women "arrived" in the decade from 1925 to 1935.

> The range of activities available to women was proportionally larger than in any other period of history. Women took up surfing, sailboat racing, speedboating, aviation, curling, polo, fencing, squash racquets, skiing, bobsledding, figure skating, speed skating, dogsled racing and even jai alia — all in addition to the more traditional activities. Furthermore, there was a growth of high level competition, with international tournaments promoted for most sports.

- - - - - - -

Middle and working class women took up sport, bringing the participation levels to record numbers (Gerber, 1973, p. 2).

Fidler (1973) investigated 435 sport and athletic organizations identified in the 1972 *Encyclopedia of Associations*. She noted men's, women's co-recreational, professional and amateur organizations whose memberships included "individuals, clubs, federations, trainers, coaches, officials, researchers, . . . " (p. 2). Of these, Fidler selected 53 for careful study. Some of her data are presented in Tables 1 and 2. The 53 organizations, their founding dates, admission dates of women are indicated insofar as facts were obtainable. Table 2 presents some comparative membership data for males and females in 1972 of a dozen organizations. According to Gerber (1973a) national sport organizations accounted for the sponsorship of competition involving 8-10 million women in the calendar year of 1972.

Fidler's research yielded 19 conclusions. I shall share just a few with you.

1. All but a very small percentage (8.6%) of the co-recreational organizations surveyed . . . admitted women members from the date of their foundings (p. 39).

10. The greatest percentage of women involved in national sports organizations were between the ages of 19 and 40 (p. 40).

11. National co-recreational sports organizations afforded men and women nearly identical opportunities for competition on varying levels, i.e., local, state, regional, national and international (p. 40).

13. With but one exception [U.S. Polo Association], all national sports organizations maintained the same aims and objectives for men and women (p. 40).

15. The majority of organizations surveyed did not recruit and pay members to serve as instructors. Those that did utilized and paid men and women on a nearly equal basis (p. 40).

Table 1

DATES PARTIALLY DEPICTING WOMEN'S INVOLVEMENT IN NATIONAL SPORTS ORGANIZATIONS IN THE UNITED STATES*

Organization	Founded	1st Women Members	1st Women Officer(s)
American Turners	1850	1950s	1969
National Rifle Association	1871	——	——
Appalachian Mountain Club	1876	1876	——
National Archery Association	1879	1879	1947
U.S. Lawn Tennis Association	1881	1889	1957
U.S. Polo Association	1890	1972	none
Amateur Fencer's League	1891	1912	——
U.S. Golf Association	1894	1894	——
North Amer. Yacht Racing Union	1897	——	none
Amateur Trapshooting Association	1900	1918	——
American Canoe Association	1900	1900	1970
U.S. Revolver Association	1904	——	——
U.S. Ski Association	1904	——	1964
American Casting Association	1906	unknown	1970
Ntl. Horseshoe Pitchers Assn.	1915	1919	——
American Tennis Association	1916	——	1961
Women's Intl. Bowling Congress+	1916		
U.S. Figure Skating Association	1921	——	——
Amateur Bicycle League of America	1921	1938	1956
U.S. Field Hockey Association+	1922		
American Motorcycle Association	1924	1924	1972
Ntl. Skeet Shooting Association	1926	1926	1970
Ntl. Duckpin Bowling Congress	1927	1927	——
U.S. Women's Squash Racquets Assn.+	1928		
U.S. Volleyball Association	1928	——	——
Soaring Society of America	1932	1932	1938
Ntl. Muzzle Loading Rifle Assn.	1933	1933	1940

Table 1 (continued)

Organization	Founded	1st Women Members	1st Women Officer(s)
Amateur Softball Association	1933	1933	1960
U.S. Table Tennis Association	1933	1933	——
American Badminton Association	1937	1937	1930s
American Platform Tennis Assn.	1937	1971	1971
American Water Ski Association	1939	1939	1957
National Field Archery Assn.	1939	——	——
American Jr. Bowling Congress	1947	1947	1964
U.S. Prof. Tennis Association	1947	1947	——
U.S. Women's Curling Assn.+	1947		
Billiard Congress of America	1948	1967	none
Eastern Tennis Patrons	1950	1950	——
Ladies' Prof. Golf Assn.+	1950		
U.S. Handball Association	1951	——	none
U.S. Judo Federation	1952	1952	none
Intl. DN Ice Yacht Racing	1953	1953	1960
Intl. Women's Fishing Assn.+	1955		
U.S. Parachute Association	1957	1957	none
Underwater Society of America	1959	——	1964
Prof. Ski Instructors of America	1960	1961	none
Los Angeles Aikido	1961	1963	1970
Prof. Archers Association	1961	1961	none
U.S. Track & Field Federation	1961	1961	——
U.S. Gymnastics Association	1963	1963	1965
Billiard Players of America	1964	——	none
U.S. Duffers Association	1965	1965	1968
American Woman's Lawn Bowls Assn.+	1970		

—— no data reported
+ all-women's organization
* SOURCE: Fidler, M. A. A survey of the nature and extent of women's involvement in selected national sports organizations. Paper presented at The Conference on Women and Sport, Western Illinois University, Macomb, Illinois, June 25, 1973.

Table 2

1972 MEMBERSHIP BY SEX
OF SELECTED SPORT ORGANIZATIONS*

Organization	Female	Members %	Male	%
U.S. Polo Assn.	4	.4	1,015	99.6
Horseshoe Pitchers Assn.	500	4.8	10,000	95.2
Amateur Bicycle League	125	4.2	2,880	95.8
American Motorcycle Assn.	54,000	30.0	126,000	70.0
U.S. Volleyball Assn.	2,646	39.6	4,045	60.4

Amer. Jr. Bowling Congress	306,000	49.5	374,000	50.5
Billiard Cong. of America	50	20.0	200	80.0
U.S. Handball Assn.	15	.9	12,000	99.1
U.S. Judo Federation	6,400	15.5	35,000	84.5
Los Angeles Aikido	13	27.1	35	72.9
U.S. Gymnastics Fed.	2,000	4.8	40,000	95.2
Billiard Players of America	19	5.0	365	95.0

* SOURCE: Fidler, M. A. A survey of the nature and extent of women's involvement in selected national sports organizations. Paper presented at The Conference on Women and Sport, Western Illinois University, Macomb, Illinois, June 25, 1973.

18. Nearly half (47.8%) of the organizations surveyed expressed problems recruiting women members (p. 41).

Before leaving Fidler's data, contemplate, for a moment, what your expectations were—prior to reviewing Tables 1 and 2—about women's affiliations with sport organizations.

Two studies of a content-analysis nature provide information that will allow me to discuss our perceptions and the media. Kennard (1973) studied 97 magazine articles concerning women athletes. She examined two different time periods: 1959-60 and 1971-72. Kennard's comparison of the nature of information-giving utilized three general interest magazines: *Newsweek, Life* and *Look;* one general sports magazine, *Sports Illustrated;* and two specific sport periodicals which are devoted to activities that have long been accepted as both men's and women's sports—*Golf Digest* and *World Tennis.* Table 3 reveals the classification of substantive content as identified by Kennard. The researcher stated:

> It is of interest to note the attention devoted to personality and behavior in comparison with actual playing performance. Heightened interest in coaching might reflect the increasing sophistication in sports techniques. Reference to the dramatic aspects of sport might signify a trend to view sport as an art form (Kennard, 1973, p. 3).

The purpose of Kennard's study was to identify the factors most emphasized in the magazines about women athletes. She concluded that *Newsweek, Life* and *Look* concentrated on actual playing performance in 1959-60. In 1971-72, they displayed an almost equal interest in the dramatic facet of performance. In both time periods, *Sports Illustrated* emphasized the personality, behavior and private life category as much as playing and sports ability. *Golf Digest* placed twice as much emphasis on personality, behavior and private life in the earlier time period and equal emphasis on these

Table 3

THE WOMAN ATHLETE IN SELECTED MAGAZINES*

Classification of substantive content+	1959-60# f	1971-72# f
Results, championships, tournaments	84	85
Personality and behavior (in or out of sport)	58	78
Performance/actual ability	72	73
Age	72	71
Information about the sport	54	67
Private life	46	55
Geographical connections (usually hometown)	40	50
Coaching	26	43
Drama, theatrics, entertainment brought to sport by the athlete	17	37
Role conflict (woman/athlete)	29	35
Clothing and adornment	16	34
Prize money/income	—	29
Physical appearance	31	27
Training	17	22
Marital status	19	20
Struggle to compete as an athlete	—	19
Mother	10	18
Feminine appearance	19	18
Woman competing in a sport for first time	—	11

+ Categories were established if content was identified at least 10 times.

Total number of articles reviewed = 97 per year.

* SOURCE: Kennard, J. A. The woman athlete in magazines. Unpublished manuscript, The University of North Carolina at Greensboro, 1973.

categories in 1971-72. In contrast with the rest of the magazines, *World Tennis* devoted most of its print to sport ability and performance in both time periods.

An interesting aspect of Kennard's study is her analysis of female symbolism in the articles. Table 4 presents these data. In her discussion, it was pointed out that:

Recorded references to parts of the body (irrelevant to sport) included hair, eyes, skin color, facial features, legs, physique, and breasts. Blonde hair was the physical characteristic most frequently cited in all the magazines. Either the majority of athletes are blonde, or more likely, blonde is the preferred hair color in this society. Though not with nearly as much frequency, eye color (generally blue) and remarks about the physique were mentioned the same number of times. In terms of facial features, dimples were most often specified. The most frequent feminine description of the athletes was "pretty" (Kennard, 1973, p. 6).

Finally, in this information-sharing portion of my presentation, Corrigan's (1972) content analysis of the most popular sports magazine in the United States, *Sports Illustrated,* is briefly reviewed. The purpose of the investigation was to identify societal acceptance of the female athlete as it might be discerned from this particular periodical. In order to show some trends, three years of the total amount of print and the number of photographs were tallied. The results are presented in Tables 5 and 6.

Corrigan also examined the word descriptions of two different aspects of behavior. These are summarized in Table 7. Clearly, by 1970, *Sports Illustrated* was not describing female athletes' behaviors in the same way it did a decade earlier. There may be some conflict here with Kennard's findings. Her report, it should be noted included 5 other publications in addition to *Sports Illustrated.*

In summary it might be said that one cannot glean a distinct image of the sportswoman as she is represented by some facts from history and the media.

Table 4

THE WOMAN ATHLETE IN SELECTED MAGAZINES*
References to Female Symbolism

Publication	1959-60		1971-72	
	f	*N/articles*	*f*	*N/articles*
Sports Illustrated	46	33	49	30
Newsweek; Life; Look	15	20	30	28
Golf Digest	10	11	10	12
World Tennis	14	33	21	27

* SOURCE: Kennard, J. A. The woman athlete in magazines. Unpublished manuscript, The University of North Carolina at Greensboro, 1973.

Table 5

SPORTS ILLUSTRATED
COVERAGE OF WOMEN ATHLETES*

Year	Articles N	Articles About Women/N	% of total
1960	420	21	5.0
1965	357	7	2.0
1970	353	7	2.0

Table 6

SPORTS ILLUSTRATED
PHOTOGRAPHS OF WOMEN ATHLETES*

Year	Photos N	Photos of Women/N	% of total
1960	2609	394	15.1
1965	1215	181	14.9
1970	1317	109	8.2

* SOURCE: Corrigan, M. Societal acceptance of the female athlete as seen through the analysis of content of a sports magazine. Unpublished manuscript, University of Massachusetts, 1972.

Table 7

SPORTS ILLUSTRATED
USE OF TERMS DESCRIBING BEHAVIOR*

1960	1965	1970

RE: *Extrovert Behavior of Female Athletes*

1960	1965	1970
friendly	friendly	vivacious
bouncy	buoyant	alive
lively	exuberant	exuberant
cheerful	expressive	versatile
bright	irresistible	nicely elegant
brilliant	frank	poised
elegant	relaxed	
enthusiastic	charming	
happy	unpredictable	
congenial	**warm**	
amiable	gracious	
self sufficient	complex	
highly strung	emotional	
volatile	ebullient	
combustible	hot tempered	
jealous	caustic	

RE: *Introvert Behavior of Female Athletes*

1960	1965	1970
steady	serene	wistful
sure	cool	ethereal air
quiet	bland	gentle
thoughtful	pristine	looking silly
levelheaded	innocuous	set apart
unassuming	self conscious	solemn
sleeply	capable	feminine
impressive	impressive	
thoroughly feminine	accomplished	
concerned with	neat and feminine	
acting like	personality of	
a female	a puppy	

wholesome	prosperous
look of gracefulness	graceful
delicate grace	extraordinary
manners of a	kindness
natural delicacy	impeccable
religious	well bred
implacable	
princess	
unpresuming queen	

* SOURCE: Corrigan, M. Societal acceptance of the female athlete as seen through the analysis of content of a sports magazine. Unpublished manuscript, University of Massachusetts, 1972.

Some Phenomena of Perception

For our purposes, let us consider perception as a human-conceived construct that describes the complicated and systematic processes of organizing knowledge and facilitating communication (Dember, 1965, p. 24). According to Hochberg (1964), "perception is one of the oldest subjects of speculation and research in the study of man (vii)." The topic has captured the energies and talents of scholars who represent various fields of knowledge, e.g., philosophy, physiology, physics. At one point in time, perception was the central issue of psychology. Indeed, intersting explanations have been offered as to why things look the way they do — from Helmholtz's (1925) notions of "unconscious inference" to Gibson's (1969) laws of differentiation and filtering. Yet, as Gibson stated, ". . . we are still a pretty long way from knowing (p. 471)."

Perceptual theorists are in agreement that individuals differ in their perceptions of situations. There is also a good degree of confidence that how input is perceived is determined by numerous factors including ". . . (a) the input, (b) principles of figure-ground organization, (c) the concepts which have been previously associated with the input, (d) the set of the perceiver, (e) on-going brain activity in the perceiver and (f) the motives of the perceiver (McKeachie and Doyle, 1966, p. 201)."

Concerning input, Fearing (1962) pointed out that in communicative behavior — such as the media reporting women's sport events — effective stimuli, the symbols, that is, are produced by human agents. Paraphrasing this idea, Smith and Smith (1966) reminded us that "they [symbols] acquire their meanings through human use, and they are used in attempts to control human situations (p. 165)." To put it in a more popular phrase, the meaning of meaning is meaning.

The perceptual phenomenon I wish to emphasize, however, is not input, per se. It is perceptual set. A well-accepted principle deriving from our ideas about perceptual set is that an individual more clearly perceives the events he or she *expects to perceive.* Solley and Murphy (1960), for example, build the notion of expectancy into their model of the perceptual act. See Table 8. What is important to this discussion of the media and women and sport about perceptual expectancy is its capability of preempting our ideation. As Maslow (1970) explained, in this world of human-devised concepts, abstractions, beliefs, stereotypes and the like, one confuses his/her hopes, fears, etc. or those of the cultural group with reality (p. 154). And this is further confounded by the motives of the perceiver; see Table 8. At the risk of both over-generalizing and over-simplifying, I remind you that what we know is, after all, the result of combining information with prior understandings and affects. If, then, we have been socialized to regard female sport involvement as unattractive, improper or role conflicting, it is highly likely that we will perceive these effects in the articles we read, the TV we view, the values we formulate . . . Actually, without even trying hard, we come to know that instrumental aggression associated with sport fulfills the need to achieve of men, that male temperaments better deal with the demands of coaching, that so-called male traits are capable of coping with the pressure of high level competition. In short, we view sport and athletics as "belonging" to the

Table 8

MODEL OF THE PERCEPTUAL ACT*

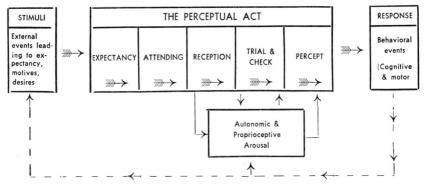

* SOURCE: Solley, C. M., and Murphy, G. *Development of The Perceptual World.* New York: Basic Books, 1960.

males of the species! And we behave accordingly to these human activities.

The Media and the Future

It would be totally inadequate for me, in closing, to merely appeal to the media to "tell it like it is" or to launch a campaign for the employment of women journalists and announcers whose perceptual expectancies would undoubtedly be different than those of *Sports Illustrated's* Joe Jares or ABC's Howard Cosell. (Look at the effects of Rosemary Casals in the broadcast booth during the King-Riggs match!)

My convictions about the information-giving role of the media in influencing the future of girls and women's sports should already be clear. I have concern about *which* events, individuals, issues and themes are reported. Also, the manner in which these are represented is equally important. To the extent that it is possible, I want, of course, unbiased and complete communication.

But above and beyond information-giving, the media is responsible for the evaluations we make of human sport endeavors. This judgmental dimension is inextricably tied to perceiving. As perceptual double-agents, the media first gets our attention; in so doing, they cause us to appraise that which is communicated. When I turn the page of a newspaper after scanning a column but not heeding its details, I have made a judgment. It is to the function of evaluation that my closing remarks are addressed.

Evaluation is a process by which the worth of something is discovered or ascertained. Undoubtedly, the media will continue to influence the value we place on sport and athletics. Therefore, conscious efforts should be exerted to contribute to meaningful and realistic evaluation. First, there needs to be recommitment to the position that reporting and evaluating are inseparable. In addition, I offer the following suggestions (with apologies to Stake and Denny, 1969). These are notions about the evaluation process which apply to sport communication.

1. Provide truthful representation of the goals and priorities of sport — in their broadest as well as most specific sense. Place these in appropriate juxtaposition to one another.

2. Devise techniques for making assessments that will encourage participation in the evaluative process by readers and audiences as well as sportsmen and sportswomen.

3. Give coverage to facts that pertain to standards and judgments or merit about sport. Do not side-step controversial or unpopular issues.

4. Synthesize the entire information processing operation by attempting to put together salient "pieces," ferreting out inconsistencies, departing from precedent when desirable, and fitting together emerging trends.

The order is a tall one. But it is one of the ways by which we may overcome our blindness to the evidences about sport that surround us.

A comment by a Canadian, Marshall McLuhan, whose ideas have been most exciting to me, brings me to my final statement. McLuhan and Fiore (1967) said "All media are extensions of some human faculty . . . All media work us over . . . Any understanding of social and cultural change is impossible without a knowledge of the way media work as environments (p. 26)." Sports and athletics are also extensions of human faculties. Likewise they work as environments. Whether these human creations can be mutually beneficial or destructive of each other is the question. The answer, I propose, is in the eyes and ears, the memory, and the emotions of the perceiver.

LIST OF SOURCES CITED

Corrigan, M., "Societal Acceptance of the Female Athlete as Seen Through the Analysis of Content of a Sports Magazine." Unpublished manuscript, University of Massachusetts, 1972.

Dember, W. N., *Psychology of Perception*. New York: Holt, 1965.

Fearing, F., "Human Communication," *Audio-Visual Communication Review*, 1962, 10 (5), pp. 78-108.

Fidler, M. A., "A Survey of the Nature and Extent of Women's Involvement in Selected National Sports Organizations," Paper presented at The Women and Sport Conference, Western Illinois University, Macomb, Illinois, June 1973.

Gerber, E. W., "Little Ms. Muffet Has Left Her Tuffet," Paper presented at the 35th Annual Conference of the New York State Association for Health, Physical Education and Recreation, Kiamesha Lake, New York, January 1973.

Gerber, E. W., Felshin, J., Berlin, P., and Wyrick, W., *The American Woman in Sport*. Reading, Massachusetts: Addison-Wesley, 1973a (In press).

Gibson, E. J., *Principles of Perceptual Learning and Development*. New York: Appleton. 1969.

Helmholtz, H. V., *Handbook of Physiological Optics, Vol. III*. Translated by J. P. C. Southall. New York: Optical-Society of America, 1925.

Hochberg, J. E., *Perception*. Englewood Cliffs, N. J.: Prentice-Hall, 1964.

Howell, N., and Howell, M. L., *Sports and Games in Canadian Life 1700 to the Present*. Toronto: Macmillan, 1969.

Kennard, J. A., "The Woman Athlete in Magazines," Unpublished manuscript, The University of North Carolina at Greensboro, 1973.

Maslow, A. H., *Motivation and Personality*. New York: Harper and Row, 1970.

McKeachie, W. J., and Doyle, C. L., *Psychology*. Reading, Massachusetts: Addison-Wesley, 1966.

McLuhan, M., and Fiore, Q., *The Medium Is the Message*. New York: Bantam, 1967.

Scott, A. F., "Making the Invisible Woman Visible," Presentation to The University Series on Women in American Life, The University of North Carolina at Greensboro, Greensboro, North Carolina, September 1973.

Solley, C. M., and Murphy, G., *Development of the Perceptual World*. New York: Basic Books, 1960.

Smith, K. U., and Smith, M. F., *Cybernetic Principles of Learning and Educational Design*. New York: Holt, 1966.

Stake, R. E., and Denny, T., "Needed Concepts and Techniques for Utilizing More Fully the Potential of Evaluation," In R. W. Tyler (Ed.) *Educational Evaluation: New Roles, New Means. The sixty-eighth yearbook of the National Society for the Study of Education, Part II*. Chicago: National Society for the Study of Education, 1969, pp. 370-390.

Jack Dulmage

Sports Editor

"The Windsor Star"

It is going to be difficult for me to stay within the context of what I have been assigned to discuss.

Given the title, the influence of the media, I am inclined to think immediately about other influences — the influence of affluence and leisure time, the influence of television as a massive indoctrination force, the influence of fast airplanes, the influence of governments at every level, the influence of the changing role of women, the influence of global standards.

I am inclined to think that these influences and not the influence of the media, excluding television which has a tremendous effect on all things, are what we have to talk about.

In the last 25 years, two things have come to pass on this continent and elsewhere that never occurred previously in the recorded history of athletics or sports.

One — the non-athlete has become a participant in some form of physical endeavor, usually organized commercially to expand his interest in a surrounding maelstrom of sport he can hardly escape from if he wanted to.

Two — The spectator has found it fashionable to patronize and make possible the expansion of any athletic activity that is regularly packaged and sold on television.

It is going to be impossible to discuss what has occurred in sport in the last quarter of a century and what will occur without paying close attention to the television industry.

There is mounting evidence that television, because of its ability to look in on, and isolate, and stress any moment of activity in any part of the world has achieved and continues to gain the power of new estate. Its decision-making, its morality, its preferences and vetoes affect all of us.

It is a well understood fact among the entrepreneurs of sport that television exposure and approval is the gateway to public acceptance, to expansion into the lush endorsement markets of commerce.

It is also the gateway to a new primacy on the scale of human events. You don't have to agree with that, but it doesn't much matter whether you do or not. The modern rule of thumb is if you're on television, you're in the bigs. That is what I call power, the power to promote the station of the little man to the once inviolate dais of captains and princes.

Television can create a league and make it rich. Or it can ignore you and injure your legacy. It can hit you over the head with enough instant replays to make you forget about the original.

It calls shots. It tells you when to start, what colors to wear, what products to praise. It pays you to the point of financial dependency.

The United States Congress recently decreed that televised professional football belongs to the public when it can't buy a ticket. The amateurs are owned by the public as well. North American television rights for the 1976 Olympic Games at Montreal were sold three years in advance for $25 million.

I mention these things in order to show that whatever we may have thought about what sport and athletics were, and were going in pre-television days, it is necessary now to examine them in the light of altogether new premises.

The would-be athlete of today still knows what a press clipping is, but he is more likely to keep his eye on television ratings.

Because the word "dilemma" occupies the thematic role of this seminar, I hasten to suggest that it ought to apply to those poles of the athletic scene which are over-ridingly in control of it — that is, television and the response to television.

Let me tell you how television has influenced the fourth estate. The beat reporter today, running several hours behind the immediacy of any televised presentation, has been compelled to penetrate into areas that didn't previously command his first interests.

He goes further off the field because if he stays on it he finds himself pre-empted by as many as seven television cameras and a battery of witness experts who usually include celebrities and privileged insiders.

Television has taken over the spectacle itself. However it provokes a great many unanswered questions, and it is the nature of reporting today to answer those questions, and to challenge when necessary the values that a visual system tyrannized by the clock and by its passing image is forced to sell.

I hope you have noticed the tremendous challenge taken up by *The Washington Post* and the *New York Times* against electronic images that have been shattered into small pieces in the Watergate calamity.

What I am saying is that in all fields of human endeavor including athletics, newspapers are only beginning to re-establish their critical powers which have been diverted, and to some extent put to sleep by the television industry.

Newspapers are retooling their machines. They are asking questions they never asked before. They are poking into corners they never went before. They are training themselves to climb over television and gain new heights. It has taken a while, but it has begun to happen. And the more it happens, the more that sports will be brought back to the people, and to those values that the people have a right to insist on.

What about those values? The thing that strikes me about athletics in 1973 is diluted complexity — the same computerized complexity that has encroached on almost every facet of our life and times.

There is some form of organized sport for every human from little children to old people, from retarded people to the so-called beautiful people, from cripples in wheel chairs to the deaf and blind, from Sam Snead and Gord Howe to Olga Korbut and Boris Spassky.

Would you believe that when I was a kid, I hung around fire halls and blacksmith shops so I could play horseshoes against old men? The only competition that was organized was a carpet ball league and euchre tournament for pot roast prizes.

When I was 16 I taught swimming, life-saving and gymnastics for $2 a week. When I was 18, I owned one badminton racquet and a used pair of roller skates. I couldn't make the basketball team because I blew History and French. Turk Broda stayed at our place one summer playing baseball. He couldn't afford to stay at the Y. When war broke out, I was making thirteen-and-a-half cents an hour as head shipper in a soft drink factory. On Sunday afternoons I knew a guy who could get the Green Bay Packers on his radio.

Three things about sports don't change — the need to win, the need to pursue excellence, and the need to have a piece of the action.

Given that, all we have to know is how, and how much we're going to teach the kids, who is going to build the play pens, and who is going to pay for everything.

In Canada we have a lot of debate about that because the open door to the United States with its immense population, markets and spending power, swings both ways, and it subordinates Canadian enterprise as surely as grapefruit are bigger than apples.

Think for a moment that in 1976 Canada is going to spend many millions of dollars floating the play pen for the Olympic Games while the United States and Russia will win most of the competitions.

Why? Image, that's why. The need to be first in something. The best in something. Canada is terribly image conscious in these times. One of the best examples of that was the Canada-Russia hockey series in 1972, an event that rocked the national soul, but was scarcely a pause in the steady torrent of talent under export to the United States.

Consider that Canada has built a monument to American baseball in Montreal — with Canadian money and American players.

Consider that the Canadian Football League is strongly tempted to burst out of its grass-roots identity cocoon and become involved with American franchises. There is fear that its major franchises and markets may first defect to the National Football League, destroying the single Canadian bastion of major sport identity.

In Canada, we have debated, and still argue whether we ought to be staging the 1976 Olympic Games. It is an honor, one supposes to reap an abundance of medals on the podium. For some countries, the principal honor is to build the podium.

How, the problem reads, can a small power country go world-class in sports without going broke? If we leave this to governments we are going to have quite traumatic happenings such as the 1972 Canada-Russia hockey series.

You will have noticed, that in consequence of that experience, the private interests of hockey have pursued their own line of trans-oceanic completition, and have failed to get past one of the first hurdles in dealing with a state-controlled operation. I refer of course to Russia's cancellation of an eight-game tour of American National Hockey League sites.

We hear a great deal these days of American sports overlords proposing global competition, global leagues, which I suppose is not so strange considering they represent business millionaires who thrive by expanding and diversifying, and who use professional sports as a vehicle on those journeys of fun and business.

The connection between sport and commerce has never been stronger than it is today. You can say that the connection between free government and free commerce has never been stronger, either.

And you can say that some governments, let us take the government of Canada for one, are determined to inspire and subsidize regional, national and international programs of physical fitness and games . . . which, I hasten to point out, are controllable, regimental and without competition in state-run societies . . . but are not thus manageable in a free society where private enterprise can prostitute them.

This dilemma, if you care to call it that, was well illustrated when the two-nation National Hockey League priced the Canadian national hockey team out of existence — whereupon the amateurs struck back by using major league professionals to confront the Russians and appease the hunger of the national soul . . . and whereupon now, no one knows for sure what business as usual is.

We have the further dilemma whereby governments have become the only auspices and agents to build major sports facilities —with public money of course—and are then forced to rent them to professionals who use them as leasing levers to set one city against another.

If you look at the North American system as a whole, you can see that we are inviting and shoving our children to grow up in a test tube of athletics, and be trained well enough to pursue world-class competition which has the Olympics as the ultimate god and goal. And that along the way, at any stage, that suits private enterprise, the products of this "Innocents Abroad" system are readily seduced to career professionalism where money has been growing increasingly on trees in recent years.

As Avery Brundage so well knew—it is a pity he was unable to accept an invitation to participate in this seminar—the Olympic Games have been growing into a house of massive commercial prostitution.

If we were to remove the Olympics, we might get rid of the international athletic rat race and its enormous governmental sponsorship. This would compel the sports industry to pay for all of its own affairs and banish the cozy lines of pretence that keep separating amateurs from professionals.

I don't expect to see it happen, and I don't think you do, either. It is the nature of a free society to produce great athletes, and the barons of commerce to exploit them.

Since this is a seminar on sport, and not commerce, and I agree we can't separate them anyway, I suggest that the rest of us understand the kind of ride we have always been along for.

We can at least expose and define, and then raise hell with the hypocrisies of our ways.

I understand that a dilemma is a situation involving choice between equally unsatisfactory alternatives.

I am certain that is one of the reasons I became a newspaper person. I can play with the alternatives without choosing them.

Discussion Period

Question

What's the reason for the major part of the sports sections of newspapers being filled with professional athletics, and very little on the amateur scene. Jim Finks stated NFL teams are in the entertainment business and why shouldn't all that be on the entertainment page?

JACK DULMAGE

Well, you get to the heart of the newspaper business when you ask questions like that, because the business of putting a newspaper together, or any part of it, is a highly discriminatory process. The biggest receptacle in the newspaper office is the wastepaper basket; and really without that you couldn't get the paper out, you couldn't put it together. You have to discriminate, you have to be brutal, you have to be ruthless almost. That means that you have to make very rapid and arbitrary decisions about what will appear in the paper and what won't appear in the paper. It involves a lot of heart-aches. If you didn't have to put the newspaper out you wouldn't do it.

And, in answer to that, you therefore have a value system or judgment system that involves the majority of so-called readership, the popular demands, the demands created by the broadcast indus-try. The people often see and hear things on the radio and tele-vision and they want it backed up. They want to see it in print. That is part of the function of the newspaper much more so today than it ever was in pre-television and in the early days of radio.

You say, "Why don't we run more stories and devote more space to minor athletics or amateur sports and things like that?" It's simply impossible. From time to time we will overemphasize a particular sport or activity in order to give it its day in court, so to speak. In the general run of things, however, when you are dealing with a news space of ten to eighteen columns a day professional sport is going to occupy the bulk of it because they do fantastically much more of it, and because they are in the public attention by other means which force us to attend to it. We can't ignore it. It's simply reader demand. It bothers us that we can't give as much attention to the other, but were we to suddenly devote the paper to an equit-able balance so to speak of all the minor sports that exist (and my heavens there are hundreds of them, you just have no idea, abso-lutely hundreds of them) our wastepaper basket would be full of things which would ring the telephone off the wall. We would be in all kinds of difficulty. So we have to respond to public pressure in that sense.

There is an area of practicality that we have to deal with here, and I am trying to explain the motivations and the judgment values that are behind the type of decision that takes place.

JEOFF GOWANS

First, what sort of data collection goes on to determine what the reader wants in the paper? And, one other comment in response, partly in support of the questioner and to Dr. Berlin's comments, I have some data here from a study which was conducted in 1969. Maybe it is getting a little old now, but thirty papers from across Canada were surveyed fairly intensely and (again with a list of generalizations) a slightly closer look at these sports reveals a few striking points:

First, they are male sports.

Second, they are professional sports.

Third, they are largely in summer, and this survey took place from May 15th to August 15th. So naturally you would expect this.

And, fourth, they are to a considerable extent played in the United States.

JAMES DUTHIE

I don't know if we ought to give Mr. Dulmage time to comment on that. I am going to go on for the moment.

Question

In your studies or the data that you reviewed was the amount of activity in sport and in the paper "directly proportioned to the severity of the economic depression of the time in North America?"

PEARL BERLIN

As far as I know the data was not examined in the light of the economic picture of the times. The answer is no.

Question

In his paper (you are answering now for Douglas Fisher), he indicated that he foresees an increased diversity in sports and sports participation in the years ahead. There is some evidence to suggest that the range of activities may be actually diminishing. In your particular role within the broad governmental spectrum of Canada and Canadian sport, how do you view the future? Diminishing or expanding?

JEOFF GOWANS

Expanding. I would term, risking the problems of definition, expanding at the recreational level.

JACK DULMAGE

I am not privy to everything Mr. Fisher has in mind for the people of Canada on behalf of the Government of Canada. I remember one time several years ago he told me there was going to be a tremendous hockey series between Canada and Russia, and I didn't believe him. So, I have been a little bit leery since in estimating the powers and predictions of Mr. Fisher who, as I say, is privy to a lot of things that I am not.

Question

How did the dominance of males in the administration and government of amateur sports of all levels effect women in sport? And, how can women have any effect on the establishment?

PEARL BERLIN

Obviously, given the approach that I took, I would have to say that it effects it markedly. It effects it in all of the experiences, and all of the stereotype perceptions, and all of the values which have been established by males for males and have been merely imposed or assumed to be pertinent to women. We have no illusions that this is not a problem that warrants some attention. The question is, "How quickly and with what help can we crawl through the experiences and go through the training processes, and establish for women an array of qualified people who could give some leadership or supplemental compliment to the male administration." I think that this is something most professional people are attempting to get at at this particular forum. I don't know.

Question

Do you think the media has any responsibility for the recent growth of individual sports such as tennis or are they just reporting on an already present trend?

JEOFF GOWANS

I would like to think that they had some responsibility for it, but I don't have any data; and, therefore, I have got to base this on the attitude or an opinion, and I think they are just reporting what is happening. I would just like to make one comment. That is, it seems to me that we are dealing with the basic problem of attitudes here. Namely, if the media thinks they are reporting what the readers want to read, then there is little likelihood of change. If the television commentator thinks he is giving the sort of information that the viewer wants, there is little likelihood of change. There is perhaps need for closer communication, maybe along these lines, for some dialogue to have a look and try to define more clearly what he has wanted. I had an unique experience last year in Munich, where on three consecutive days I was able to watch German television; British television both (BBC and ITV); and then the following day quite disastrously Canadian television. Reporting on the games and the difference in the content was quite remarkable. The British commentator happened to be doing a session on the women's discus and the men's high jump. And, he made no apologies for talking about such things as applying force and free leg swing and so on, because clearly he felt that he had some educational responsibility.

If a Canadian commentator knew what free leg swing was or what application of force was, it would amaze me. And, secondly, if he did it, he would probably be sacked or fired for swearing on the media.

One of the basic questions that I would ask is, "What responsibility do the media feel they have for educating the public?"

The Canadian public by and large (and again this is opinion) is unsophisticated sportswise. Those of you who were in Munich and watched the crowds in there (admittedly by a sample, because they had gone there because they had some deep interest in the games) would appreciate the differences between that crowd and the average crowd who attend a sporting meet here. They knew every single move that was going on. They were in total empathy with the whole situation. Now, I think this has some relationship to that which is put on the air or put in print.

Maybe the problem is because we have so many newspapers in Canada. We are very very thin on the ground in terms of having people in the media with appropriate backgrounds which enable them to produce this analytical approach. And, I would like some reaction on that.

PEARL BERLIN

Well, I am in complete agreement with him and tried to hit it from another point. I think I called his approach, in my own terms, the evaluation process. I want to make the press, the media, total media responsible (and I am sorry Mr. Fisher isn't here so I cannot disagree with him openly in terms of the mere information-giving aspect that he foresees the role to be). One of the things I would like to emphasize is that these people do have responsibility, and what I would call for is that they take it fully and they admit it. Do the job with this end in mind—offering some critical evaluation.

Question

In terms of amateur sport if we can use terms like this. By and large from the panel quick responses: "Media, beneficial or harmful — functional or disfunctional?"

JACK DULMAGE

I could say yes to some, and no to other parts. I may be biased, it is beneficial. Anything that we do for amateur sport is beneficial.

PEARL BERLIN

I think that the media can be beneficial. I don't know that they have been or not. I don't know what the effects are by not educating, by not evaluating. I don't know if the pattern has been established. They have contributed to the sport or the recreational interests of people.

JEOFF GOWANS

Beneficial is that they give it coverage, but I agree with the evaluative need. On the other hand, it is a two-way street. They have responsibilities too, and the main media gripes about the problems of amateur sport. First of all, many of the amateur sport executives are never available to the media. They are most uncooperative. And, secondly, there is a great lack of personal contact, and therefore, the information isn't fed to the media as they would like it to be fed to them. And, thirdly, there is lack of notification of events so that the media doesn't know whether they should send somebody to attend something because they don't know whether it is on or not. Fourthly, there is a lack of resource materials so that when a team goes away the media don't know any details about this team. They don't know who is going, they don't know where they live, they don't know where their home town is, they don't know where they are staying in the foreign city, where they are competing. They fail to provide adequate facilities for the media to operate during events. In many cases they almost have to break their way in to report an event. Sixth, there is a lack of accessibility to amateur athletes. Where some amateur athletes are almost locked away so that the media can't get at them, and there is probably another side to that story too. And, seventh, there is a lack of general information flow to the media. In other words, there is a lack of coordination and poor P.R. work.

So, I think that we have to look at both sides of it, and those people who are in amateur executive position had better shape up on this.